TABLE OF CONTENTS

Top 20 Test Taking Tips

1. Carefully follow all the test registration procedures
2. Know the test directions, duration, topics, question types, how many questions
3. Setup a flexible study schedule at least 3-4 weeks before test day
4. Study during the time of day you are most alert, relaxed, and stress free
5. Maximize your learning style; visual learner use visual study aids, auditory learner use auditory study aids
6. Focus on your weakest knowledge base
7. Find a study partner to review with and help clarify questions
8. Practice, practice, practice
9. Get a good night's sleep; don't try to cram the night before the test
10. Eat a well balanced meal
11. Know the exact physical location of the testing site; drive the route to the site prior to test day
12. Bring a set of ear plugs; the testing center could be noisy
13. Wear comfortable, loose fitting, layered clothing to the testing center; prepare for it to be either cold or hot during the test
14. Bring at least 2 current forms of ID to the testing center
15. Arrive to the test early; be prepared to wait and be patient
16. Eliminate the obviously wrong answer choices, then guess the first remaining choice
17. Pace yourself; don't rush, but keep working and move on if you get stuck
18. Maintain a positive attitude even if the test is going poorly
19. Keep your first answer unless you are positive it is wrong
20. Check your work, don't make a careless mistake

Inorganic Chemistry

Matter

Matter is defined as anything that occupies space and has mass. Categories of matter include atoms, elements, molecules, compounds, substances and mixtures.

- An atom is the basic unit of an element that can enter into a chemical reaction.
- An element is a substance that cannot be separated into simpler substances by chemical means.
- A molecule is the smallest division of a compound that can exist in a natural state.
- A compound is a substance composed of atoms of two or more elements chemically united in fixed proportions.
- A substance is a form of matter that has a definite or constant composition and distinct properties.
- A mixture is a combination of two or more substances in which the substances retain their unique identities.

Physical and chemical properties of matter

If a property of a substance can be observed and measured without change it is a physical property. Density, melting point and boiling point are examples of physical properties. If a chemical change must be carried out in order to observe and measure a property, then the property is a chemical property. For example, when hydrogen gas is burned in oxygen, it forms water. This is a chemical property of hydrogen because after burning a different chemical substance – water – is all that remains. The hydrogen cannot be recovered from the water by means of a physical change such as freezing or boiling.

States of matter

The three states in which matter can exist are as a solid, liquid or gas. They differ from each other in the distance of separation between the individual molecules. In a solid, the molecules are very close to each other with little range of motion. Molecules in a liquid, while close, have a greater degree of freedom than molecules in a solid and can move around each other. In a gas, the molecules are separated by distances that are very large in comparison to the size of the molecules. The three states of matter can be interchanged by the addition or removal of heat. For example, when a solid is heated to its melting point, it will form a liquid. Upon further heating to its boiling point it will form a gas.

Characteristic properties
The table below outlines the characteristic properties of the three states of matter:

Gas
  Volume/shape: Assumes volume and shape of its container

Density: Low
Compressibility: High
Molecular Motion: Very free motion

Liquid
Volume/shape: Volume remains constant but it assumes shape of its container
Density: High
Compressibility: Slightly
Molecular Motion: Move past each other freely

Solid:
Volume/shape: Definite volume and shape
Density: High
Compressibility: Incompressible
Molecular Motion: Vibrates around fixed positions

Properties of liquid

Liquids have definite volumes, however, they are unable to change shape by flowing. Liquids and solids have similarities in that in each the particles touch but they can move around. This means the density of liquids will be near that of a solid. Because liquid molecules can move, they assume the shape of their container. Specific liquid properties include viscosity, or the resistance of a liquid to flow. Surface tension, when there is an attraction between the molecules of the liquid that causes the surface to act as a thin and elastic film that is under tension, is another property. This property is what causes the formation of water into spherical drops. Vapor pressure is the pressure a solid or liquid exerts when at equilibrium with its vapor at a particular temperature. Boiling point is when atmospheric pressure equals the boiling point.

Density of water

In the solid state, water is less dense than in the liquid state. This can be observed quite simply by noting that an ice cube floats at the surface of a glass of water. Were this not the case, ice would not form on the surface of lakes and rivers in those regions of the world where the climate produces temperatures below the freezing point. If water behaved as other substances, lakes and rivers would freeze from the bottom up and be detrimental to many forms of aquatic life. The lower density of ice occurs because of a combination of the unique structure of the water molecule and hydrogen bonding. In the case of ice, each oxygen atom is bound to four hydrogen atoms, two covalently and two by hydrogen bonds. This forms an ordered, roughly tetrahedral structure that prevents the molecules from getting close to each other. As such, there are empty spaces in the structure that account for the low density of ice.

Crystalline solids

The atoms of solids are closely packed and are not compressible. Since all solids have some thermal energy, the atoms vibrate. The movement is very small and rapid and cannot be seen under normal circumstances. The four types of crystalline solids have a specific melting point and contain bonds that are ionic.

- 6 -

Sodium chloride is an example. Covalent solids appear as one large molecule that is made up of a virtually limitless number of covalent bonds. Graphite is an example. Molecular solids are represented as repetitive units that consist of molecules such as ice. Metallic solids are also repeating units. They contain metal atoms. The valence electrons in metals can jump from one atom to another.

Amorphous solids

Amorphous solids have no definite melting point nor do they have regular repeating units. These are solids with no long-range order in positioning of the atoms. This is unlike atoms in crystalline solids. Window glass is an example of amorphous solids. Many polymers such as polystyrene are also amorphous. These solids may exist in two separate states. One is a "rubbery" state. The other is a "glassy" state. The transition temperature between the rubbery and glassy states is known as their glass transition temperature (Tg). More specifically, it is a temperature at which a loss of flexibility becomes lost in adhesives. Adhesives will become hard and inflexible. Adhesives which reach the Tg may fail if they are flexed. The actual temperature widely varies from 105 degrees C to less than 0 degrees C.

Plasma

Plasma is an ionized gas. It is a gas in which enough energy is provided to free the electrons from atoms and molecules. This allows both ions and electrons to coexist. Plasma can be viewed as a cloud of protons, neutrons and electrons in which the electrons detach from their molecules and atoms. This enables the plasma to act as a whole rather than a conglomerate of atoms. More than 99 percent of the visible universe is made up of plasma, most of which is visible, making it the most common state of matter. Plasma is naturally-occurring. It is what makes up the sun, the core of stars and is also found in quasars.

Thermoplastic

Thermoplastic material are materials that are plastic, melts to a liquid when it is heated and freezes into a glassy state whenever it is sufficiently cooled. Most thermoplastics are polymers with high molecular weights whose chains are associated through weak van der Waals forces such as polyethylene, stronger dipole-dipole interaction and hydrogen bonding such as nylon as well as the stacking of aromatic rings such as with polystyrene. Thermoplastic polymers are unlike "thermosetting" polymers such as vulcanized rubber which cure through added energy to a stronger form and can never be remelted or remolded once they are formed. Many thermoplastic materials are so-called "addition polymers" which are vinyl chain-growth polymers such as polypropylene.

Fifth state of matter

A condition in which atoms collapse into a single quantum state is called "Bose condensation" or "Bose-Einstein condensation." It is known as a possible fifth state of matter. Bose-Einstein condensate has been thought of by scientists as plasma's opposite. It is found at extremely low temperatures that are almost to the point where atoms do not move. The Bose-Einstein condensate consists of a phase of gaseous superfluid that has been formed by atoms and has been cooled to temperatures near absolute zero. The phenomenon was forecasted in the 1920s by Satyendra Bose and Albert Einstein.

Subatomic particles

The three subatomic particles are the proton, electron and neutron. Protons are the positively charged particles in the nucleus, with a mass of 1.67252 x 10-24 g. This is approximately 1840 times the mass of the oppositely charged electron. Neutrons are also present in the nucleus, are electrically neutral and have a mass slightly greater than that of protons. The table below summarizes the three particles:

Particle	Mass (g)	Charge
Electron	9.1095 × 10-28	-1
Proton	1.67252 × 10-24	+1
Neutron	1.67497 ×	0

Shells

Interactions between electrons are what cause the chemical behavior of atoms. Electrons of atoms remain with certain, predictable configurations of electrons.

Quantum mechanics determine the configuration of electrons in what is the atom's electric potential. The principal quantum number determines the particular electron shells with energy levels that are distinct. Usually the higher a shell's energy level is, the farther it is away from the nucleus. Valence electrons in the outermost shell have the most influence on chemical behavior. Core electrons, those not in the outer shell, have a role that usually is along the lines of a secondary effect because of screening the positive charge in the atomic nucleus.

Nucleon properties

Nucleon is the name for the two baryons (subatomic particles), the neutron and the proton. They are constituents of atomic nuclei and were thought to be elementary particles as late as the 1960s, their interaction then defined strong interactions. They now are known to be composite particles made of gluons and quarks. Constituent protons and neutrons of the atomic nucleus are known as nucleons. They are held together by a strong nuclear force in the nucleus. Nuclei transformation can play a part in radioactivity. Nuclear transformation also occurs in nuclear reactions. In nuclear fusion, two light nuclei merge into a single nucleus that is heavier. In nuclear fission, a single large nucleus divides into two or more smaller nuclei.

Electron mobility

Electrons are accelerated in an electric field, E, in an opposite direction to that field due to its negative charge. The force that acts on the electron is -eE, where e is the charge. This force causes a constant acceleration in that in the absence of obstacles in a vacuum, the electron goes continuously faster in an electric field. In solids, a different situation occurs; the electrons scatter due to collisions with atoms and vacancies that drastically change the direction in which they move. So, electrons move randomly. But they also move with a net drift that is in the opposite direction to the electric field. This drift velocity is constant and is equal to the electrical field multiplied by a constant known as the mobility, m.

$V_a = m_e E$

Electron configuration

Electron configuration, in atomic physics, is how electrons in an atom, molecule, or other body are arranged. Expressly, it is the electron placement into atomic, molecular, or other forms of electron orbitals. The state of an atom's electrons is given by four quantum numbers. Three integers are properties of the atomic orbital in which it is located. No two electrons in one atom may possess the same set of these four quantum numbers as in the Pauli exclusion principle. A standard notation is used to describe atomic electron configurations; a subshell is written in the form nx^e, where n is the shell number, x is the subshell, and e is the number of electrons present in the shell.

Unit cells

A unit cell is the smallest structure that repeats itself via translation through a crystal. These are symmetrical units that have hard spheres. Most common among unit cells are the faced-centered cubic, hexagonal close-packed and body-centered cubic. Properties that are important in unit cells are:

- The type of atoms and their radii R.
- Cell dimensions -- side a in cubic cells, side of base a and height c in hexagonal cells, in terms of R.
- n, number of atoms per unit cell. A fraction of the atom, $1/m$, is counted for an atom that is shared with m adjacent unit cells.
- CN, coordination number, the number of closest neighbors to which atoms bond.
- APF, the atomic packing factor. This is the fraction of the volume of the cell that is occupied by hard spheres. APF = Sum of atomic volumes/volumes of cell.

Plum pudding model

J.J. Thomson suggested the arrangement of protons and electrons within an atom were a "plum pudding" model. Thomson, who discovered the electron before the proton or neutron, hypothesized that an atom has electrons that are encompassed by a blob of positive charges that surround it like pudding. The electrons were believed to be positioned uniformly inside the atom and was also said to sometimes possess a cloud of positive

- 9 -

charge. By studying electricity that passed through gases, Thomson found that all atoms have certain particles, called electrons, and that they carry a negative charge. Since atoms are electrically neutral there must be positive charges somewhere in the atom to balance the electrically negative ones. This model was later disproved.

Geiger-Marsden experiment

An experiment by Hans Geiger and Ernest Marsden (under the supervision of Ernest Rutherford) at the University of Manchester led to disproving Thomson's plum pudding model of the atom. Geiger and Marsden measured the deflection of alpha particles that were directed normally onto a sheet of thin gold foil. Thomson's model would have seen the alpha particles all being deflected by at most a few degrees. But they saw a very small percentage of particles were deflected through angles that were much larger than 90 degrees. This led to additional findings later by Rutherford that suggested the atom had a very small positive charge which was able to repel the alpha particles if they were close enough.

Size and speed of atoms

Electron clouds do not have a sharp cutoff, so the size of an atom is hard to define. When atoms form crystal lattices, the distance between the centers of the adjacent atoms can be found by X-ray diffraction. This gives an estimate of the size of an atom. The radius at which the valence shells are most likely to be seen can be used for an atom. Temperature of an atom collection is measured by the average energy of motion of the atoms. Kinetic energy of the particles in the system increase as temperature increases and speeds up the motion. At room temperature, atoms that form gases in the air will move at speed of about 500 m/s or 1,100 mph.

Chemical changes

Experience and observation are necessary in order to identify chemical changes. Signs to look for include a change in color, the formation of solids, the formation of bubbles, heat and/or flame is produced or heat is absorbed. Some changes that are not chemical include the freezing or boiling of water, which are physical changes. Adding a solid to the water such as sodium chloride and it dissolving is a chemical change. This is even though the sodium chloride will disappear because if most of the water evaporates then most of the sodium chloride is recovered. The important factor in determining a chemical change is the formation of a new substance.

Oxidation of iron

Iron has the ability to rust under the right conditions which is a chemical property. Rusting is a slow chemical change. This is because rust is an iron oxide. It has different properties than iron metal. This can be illustrated by imagining steel wool burning in a fast reaction with oxygen, then contrast it with the slow rusting of iron which is also oxygenated. In iron, the element, only the atoms of iron are contacting one another. In the element oxygen, each oxygen atom is joined together to form a diatomic molecule. There is a rearranging of the atoms and molecules so that two iron atoms are combined with three oxygen atoms. This forms a completely new compound.

Distillation and fractional distillation

Distillation is the process by which different components of a mixture may be separated. Because substances in the mixture have different boiling points, some are vaporized as the temperature rises, leaving others in the liquid state. The vapors may be trapped and condensed to return them to a liquid or solid state. Fractional distillation is similar but uses a different experimental apparatus. A tower is attached to a flask containing the mixture to be distilled. As vapors rise, they are trapped and condensed, returning to the flask to repeat the process. On an industrial scale, the refinement of crude oil is based on fractional distillation; different substances such as gasoline, kerosene, and diesel are produced as rising vapors cool and condense at different temperatures.

Vaporization

The evaporation of part of a liquid will see cooling of the liquid left behind. That is because it has to extract the needed heat of vaporization from the liquid so it can change into a gaseous state. It is an important mechanism in heat transfer.

The human body is cooled when it has ambient temperatures that are above the normal body temperature. Evaporation is an effective method of cooling because of the large heat of vaporization of water. The human body cools off by perspiring to give energy, even though the temperature around the body is a higher than that of the body. The cooling rate for a liquid that is below boiling will see of heat of a vaporization change with temperature and the rate of evaporation will depend upon the relative humidity and ambient temperature.

BLEVE

A boiling liquid expanding vapor explosion (BLEVE) is a danger in many railroad accidents in which flammable chemicals are involved. It is an explosion that happens when a vessel, such as a railroad tank car, fails and inside the vessel is a liquid at a temperature well above its boiling point at normal atmospheric pressure. With such a failure, boiling can occur instantly depending on the particular boiling point of the liquid. This causes the vaporization of a large amount of the liquid to occur. If the liquid's temperature is higher than the superheat limit, then boiling of an instantaneous nature happens. If the temperature is below that limit, the energy for blast and fragmentation generation is released. This mainly comes from vapor expanding in the space above the liquid. In either instance, if the container is burning the metal is heated and this causes a loss of mechanical strength.

Vacancy and interstitials

A vacancy is a position on a lattice that is vacant due to a missing atom. It comes about upon formation of the solid. Other vacancies can be made and also take place naturally through thermal vibrations. An interstitial is an atom occupying a place outside the normal position on a lattice. It might be an impurity atom or a self-interstitial atom, which is the same as other. With vacancy and interstitials, a change in coordination of atoms around the defect takes place. This means forces are not balanced for other atoms in the solid in the same way. This results in a lattice distortion around the defect. The number of vacancies from thermal agitation follows:

$$NV = NA \times \exp(-QV/kT)$$

Where NV = total number of atoms in the solid, QV is the amount of energy needed to form vacancies, k is Boltzmann constant and T is Kelvin temperature.

Impurities in solids

All solids that are real are impure. Impurities are often added to materials in order to make the properties better. For example, carbon added in small amounts to iron produces steel. Boron impurities added to silicon causes a drastic change in its electrical properties. Solid solutions are made of a host, a solvent or matrix, which dissolves the solute. The ability to dissolve is solubility. Solid solutions have certain characteristics such as being homogeneous, maintaining crystal structure, containing randomly dispersed impurities which are either substituted or interstitial. For high solubility there must be a atom size that is similar, have similar crystal structure, possess electronegativity that is similar and have a similar valence.

Energy band structures

Atoms coming together and forming a solid have valence electrons interacting due to Coulomb forces. They also feel the electric field their own nucleus produces and that of other atoms as well. Two specific quantum mechanical effects also occur; first, through Heisenberg's uncertainty principle, electrons constrained to a small volume see its energy rise, or promotion; second, because of the Pauli exclusion principle there are limits to the number of electrons having the same property. Accordingly, the valence electrons of atoms make valence bands that are wide when forming a solid. These bands are kept apart by gaps where electrons cannot exist. In insulators and semiconductors, there are filled valence bands. No more electrons can be added, as per Pauli's principle. Electrical conduction needs electrons that can gain energy in an electric field. Since it would imply the electrons are promoted into the forbidden band gap, this is not possible.

Mössbauer effect

Rudolf Mössbauer discovered the physical phenomenon later named the Mössbauer effect in 1957. It describes the resonant and recoil free emission and absorption of gamma rays by atoms bound in a form that is solid. Mössbauer observed resonance in solid iridium, which led to the question of why gamma ray resonance was not possible in gases, but were possible in solids. Mössbauer postulated that for atoms bound into a solid, under certain conditions, a fraction of the nuclear events could take place virtually without recoil. His observation was attributed to this recoil-free fraction of nuclear events. Emitted gamma rays correspond to nuclear transition energy minus energy lost to recoil during atom emission. If the recoil energy is small then the gamma ray energy still corresponds to the nuclear transition energy and the gamma ray can be absorbed by a second atom of the type of the first. This is called resonance.

Mass balance

Mass balance is the enumeration of material that enters and leaves a system. The balance works on the conservation of mass principle in that matter cannot be created or disappear. Mass that enters a system must either leave or accumulate within the system:

$$IN = OUT + ACC$$

where IN means what is entering the system, OUT represents what leaves the system and ACC means accumulation within the system. Mass balances often are developed for total mass that crosses a system's boundaries but they may also focus on a particular element or chemical compound. When a mass balance is written for a specific compound instead of for total mass of the system, a production term (PROD) comes into play so that:

$$IN + PROD = OUT + ACC$$

The production term may then describe chemical reaction rates or other factors. PROD might be positive or negative just as is the case for ACC.

Ionization and solubilizing groups

Ionization is a term used in various ways in chemistry, all revolving around the behavior and properties of charged particles, or ions. For solutions, ionization refers to dissolved polar solutes; their separated ions, e.g. Na^+ and Cl^-, are separated from each other by molecules of solvent. This solution ionization is the basis for solution chemistry. A solubilizing group is a group or portion of a molecule that acts to increase the solubility of the molecule to which it is attached. Such groups usually act by polarizing the molecule, or specific regions of it, allowing it to interact more freely with solvent molecules of similar polarity. This concept is particularly important in organic chemistry because many vital hydrocarbon chains are not water soluble. They become water soluble, however, when a functional group such as carboxyl is attached.

Molecular structure of compounds

The molecular structures of salts, oxides, peroxides, acids, and bases are:
- Salts: In binary compounds, formed of any metal and any non-metal. In ternary compounds, formed of a metal and a complex ion.
- Oxides: any metal and oxygen.

- 13 -

- Peroxides: oxides containing one more oxygen atom than normal valence rules would predict.
- Acids: In binary compounds, hydrogen and any non-metal in solution; in ternary compounds, hydrogen and a complex ion in solution. In reactions, acids can gain or bond with an H ion.
- Bases: A ternary compound made of any metal and the complex ion OH-. Bases can lose H ions in reactions. Acids and bases together form a class of reactions called neutralization reactions. These reactions are important in many industrial and biological processes.

Periodic table

The periodic table is a tabular arrangement of the elements and is organized according to periodic law. The properties of the elements depend on their atomic structure and vary with atomic number. In the periodic table, the elements are arranged by atomic number in horizontal rows called periods and vertical columns called groups or families. They are further categorized as metals, metalloids, or nonmetals. The majority of known elements are metals; there are seventeen nonmetals and eight metalloids. Metals are situated at the left end of the periodic table, nonmetals to the right and metalloids between the two.

Periodicity
Periodicity describes the predictable and incremental nature of elements' properties and places them on the periodic table accordingly. An atom of every element has unique properties such as number of electrons, density, and mass. The periodic table is arranged such that elements near each other are more alike in these properties than those that are far apart on the table. Periodicity enables the prediction of properties and atomic configurations based on known trends represented by the position of elements on the table. One such trend is the number of electrons; reading from left to right on any given row of the table, each element contains one more electron than the one immediately preceding it. On row 4, for example, K contains 19 electrons and the next element, Ca, contains 20.

Important information and how to read
Most periodic tables contain the element's atomic weight, number, and symbol in each box. The position of an element in the table reveals its group, its block, and whether it is a representative, transition, or inner transition element. Its position also shows the element as a metal, nonmetal, or metalloid. For the representative elements, the last digit of the group number reveals the number of outer-level electrons. Roman numerals for the A groups also reveal the number of outer level electrons within the group. The position of the element in the table reveals its electronic configuration and how it differs in atomic size from neighbors in its period or group. In this example, Boron has an atomic number of 5 and an atomic weight of 10.811. It is found in group 13, in which all atoms of the group have 3 valence electrons; the

group's Roman numeral representation is IIIA.

Features and structure

The most important feature of the table is its arrangement according to periodicity, or the predictable trends observable in atoms. The arrangement enables classification, organization, and prediction of important elemental properties. The table is organized in horizontal rows called Periods, and vertical columns called Groups or Families. Groups of elements share predictable characteristics, the most important of which is that their outer energy levels have the same configuration of electrons. For example, the highest group is group 18, the noble gases. Each element in this group has a full complement of electrons in its outer level, making the reactivity low. Elements in periods also share some common properties, but most classifications rely more heavily on groups. A typical periodic table shows the elements' symbols and atomic number, the number of protons in the atomic nucleus. Some more detailed tables also list atomic mass, electronegativity, and other data.

Elements and blocks

Elements are arranged in blocks on the table in addition to being classified by periods and groups. The two groups at the left of the table are the s block, groups 3-12 are the d block, groups 13-18 are the p block, and periods 4f and 5f are the f block. Representative elements are those occupying the s and p blocks. Transition elements are those occupying the d block.

Inner transition elements are those occupying the f block. The names, "representative", "transition", and "inner transition" refer to the electron configuration of each element's atoms. The representative elements each have from one to six electrons in the outer energy levels. The transition elements have electron configurations that describe the filling of different sublevels, thereby transitioning from the s block to the p block.

Chemical reactivity

Reactivity refers to the tendency of a substance to engage in chemical reactions. If that tendency is high, the substance is said to be highly reactive, or to have high reactivity. Because the basis of a chemical reaction is the transfer of electrons, reactivity depends upon the presence of uncommitted electrons which are available for transfer. Periodicity allows us to predict an element's reactivity based on its position on the periodic table. High numbered groups on the right side of the table have a fuller complement of electrons in their outer levels, making them less likely to react. Noble gases, on the far right of the table, each have eight electrons in the outer level, with the exception of He, which has two. Because atoms tend to lose or gain electrons to reach an ideal of eight in the outer level, these elements have very low reactivity.

Groups and periods

Reading left to right within a period, each element contains one more electron than the one preceding it. (Note that H and He are in the same period, though nothing is between them and they are in different groups.) As electrons are added, their attraction to the nucleus increases, meaning that as we read to the right in a period, each atom's electrons are more densely compacted, more strongly bound to the nucleus, and less likely to be pulled away in reactions. As we read down a group, each successive atom's outer electrons are less tightly bound to the nucleus, thus increasing their reactivity, because the principal energy levels are increasingly full as we move downward within the group. Principal energy levels shield the outer energy levels from nuclear attraction, allowing the valence electrons to react. For this reason, noble gases farther down the group can react under certain circumstances.

Atomic radius

The radius of an atom is basically understood as the distance between the center of its nucleus and the outer energy level of electrons. Atomic radii are of course incredibly small and are measured in nanometers ($1nm = 10^{-9}$ m). The radius of an element tends to increase reading downward within a period because the outer energy electrons are further from the nucleus due to the shielding effect of lower energy levels. The radius of an element tends to decrease reading from left to right within a period because of the increasing charge. Recall that each subsequent element in a period has one additional proton and one additional electron. Since the positive charge of the nucleus and the negative charge of the outer energy level have both increased,

with no increase in shielding, the results are a stronger attraction and a smaller radii.

Electron configuration and ionization energy

Electron configuration is a description of how an atom's electrons are distributed throughout its energy levels and sub-levels. The energy level, sub-level, and number of electrons are represented with numbers and letters. For example, H has one electron in one energy level; its electron configuration is represented: $1s^2$. More complex atoms with higher atomic numbers have more complex configurations and notations, but the configuration is predictable based on the element's location on the periodic table. Ionization energy, or potential, is the energy required to separate electrons from their atoms, creating ions. Electrons will not separate from the atoms to which they are bound without some force acting upon them. Ionization energy is one of the trends exhibited in the periodic table; it decreases reading from top to bottom within a group, and increases reading from left to right within a period.

Electronegativity

The electron attracting power of an atom is its electronegativity and this determines a large part of its chemical behavior. Electronegativity is measured on a scale from 0 to 4 (weakest to strongest). The most electronegative elements are listed to the right of the periodic table. Conversely, those elements with low electronegativities are found at the left of the periodic table. In general, electronegativity decreases going down each group in the periodic table.

Electronegativity refers to the ability of an atomic nucleus to attract electrons when covalently bonded in molecules. In certain circumstances, one atom of a molecule may exert a stronger attraction upon a shared pair of electrons than the other atom sharing the same pair. The unequal sharing results in the shared pair being pulled closer to the nucleus of the "stronger" atom. For example, in a molecule of hydrogen chloride, the shared electrons are pulled closer to the nucleus of the Cl atom, resulting in a slight negative charge of the atom and a corresponding slightly positive charge of the H. The shared electrons do not leave the covalent bond; they are merely pulled closer to the Cl nucleus showing greater electronegativity in Cl than in H. Electronegativity is a trend predicted by the periodic table; it increases reading upward within a group and left to right within a period.

The Pauling scale is a system of measuring electronegativity (written by Linus Pauling in 1932). The scale assigns ascending numerical values to represent electronegativity, with the lowest at .7 (francium) and the highest at 3.98 (fluorine). Simple subtraction yields the difference between electronegativity of elements in a compound (represented as σEN), which in turn allows predictions about types and strengths of bonds likely to be formed. Ionic bonds are characterized by large σEN values, while covalent bonds will have very little to no

difference in electronegativity. The Mulliken scale is another system for measuring electronegativity (devised by Robert Mulliken in 1934). Rather than arbitrarily assigning beginning and ending points, however, this scale's electronegativity values are the average of an element's ionization potential and electron affinity. The result is shown in electron volts.

Chemical bonds

Most chemical bonds can be classified as either ionic or covalent. Metals typically contain fewer valence electrons than nonmetals and form ionic bonds with other metals. The type of bond likely to be present in a compound can be predicted by the position of the elements on the periodic table. The metals are found in groups 1-12 of the periodic table (though H is not a metal). Elements within these groups will tend to form ionic bonds with one another because fewer valence electrons are available for sharing. The nonmetals are found in the right 1/3 of the table, or groups 13-18. Because they have more valence electrons available for sharing, they tend to form covalent bonds both in bonding with other nonmetals and with metals.

Neutrons in atom models

Atoms that have similar outer electrons also have similar properties and their chemical properties take place on a repeating basis. The periodic table arranges the elements so that atoms with the same number of outer electrons are above each other in the table. The first column of the table, the metals, includes all the elements whose atoms have only one loosely bound outer electron. The last column, the noble gases, has all the elements whose atoms have no outer electrons. Protons and neutrons attract each other via a strong nuclear force. This force works only between those nucleons that are neighbors while an electric repulsion is long range but only works between protons. Adding neutrons to the nucleus increase the amount of strong force without an increase in the electric repulsion.

Elemental symbols

Many element symbols are the first letter of the element capitalized, such as "O" for oxygen, "S" for sulfur and "H" for hydrogen. Since more elements exist than letters of the alphabet and the names of several elements begin with the same letter, the symbolizing must be varied; The symbols may also be the first letter of the element capitalized followed by the second letter of the element such as "Al" for aluminum and "Ba" for barium. Since some of the elements have the same first and second letters, for example calcium and cadmium, the element symbol may be the first letter capitalized followed by the third letter of the element "Ca" for calcium or "Cd" for cadmium. Non-English words are also chosen as elemental symbols such as "K" for potassium, from the German "kalium"; "Fe" for iron, from the Latin "ferrum"; "Cu" for copper, from the Latin "cuprum"; and "Ag" for silver, from the Latin word "argentum."

Properties of metals

Some of the characteristic properties of metals are as follows:
- Most metals are malleable and can be pounded into thin sheets; most are also ductile which means they can be drawn out into thin wires.
- All metals are solid at room temperature with the exception of Mercury, which is a liquid at room temperature.
- Metals usually have low ionization energies and they normally lose electrons in chemical reactions. Compounds consisting of metals <u>and</u> non-metals are usually ionic.
- Most metal oxides are basic oxides and those that will dissolve in water form metal hydroxides:
- Metal oxide + water -> metal hydroxide
- $Na_2O(s) + H_2O(l) -> 2NaOH(aq)$
- $CaO(s) + H_2O(l) -> Ca(OH)_2(aq)$
- Metal oxides show their basic chemical nature by reacting with acids and forming salts and water.
- Metal oxide + acid -> salt + water
- $MgO(s) + HCl(aq) -> MgCl_2(aq) + H_2O(l)$
- $NiO(s) + H_2SO_4(aq) -> NiSO_4(aq) + H_2O(l)$

Mass

Mass is a property of a physical object quantifying the amount of matter it contains. The mass of an object, unlike weight, stays the same regardless of its physical location. Inertial mass is a measure of the resistance of an object to changing its state of motion when a force is applied. An object with small inertial mass changes its motion more readily and an object that has a large internal mass does not change as readily. Passive gravitational mass refers to the measure of the strength of an object's interacting with the gravitational field. Within a gravitational field an object with a smaller passive gravitational mass will experience a smaller force than an object possessing a larger passive gravitational mass. This force is called the weight of the particular object. Active gravitational mass measures the strength of the gravitational field because of a particular object.

Atomic mass scale

Atoms of different elements all have different masses. In early research, it was found that separating 100 grams of water into its basic elements resulted in 11.1 grams of hydrogen and 88.9 grams of oxygen. Once it was later discovered that water has two atoms of hydrogen for every atom of oxygen, which implied that an oxygen atom must weigh about 16 times as much as a hydrogen atom. To have a base unit of measurement, scientists developed the atomic mass unit (amu), and standardized it against the 12C isotope of carbon (amu = 12). Using this unit of measurement, the mass of the hydrogen atom (1H) is 1.0080 amu and the mass of an oxygen atom (16O) is 15.995 amu. Once the masses of atoms were determined, the amu could be assigned an actual value:

Average atomic mass

- 1 amu = 1.66054 x 10-24 grams

or conversely:

- 1 gram = 6.02214 x 1023 amu

The average atomic mass of each element is also referred to as its atomic weight, which is listed in the periodic table.

Molecular weight

Molecular weight equals the sum of atomic weights of the atoms in the molecule. To calculate molecular weight, find the average weight or mass of the elements listed in the periodic table. The mass can be determined by knowing their particular molecular formula. For example, the weight of Methane, or CH_4, can be determined as such:
MW{Methane} = (1 carbon atom per molecule)*(12.011 grams per mole for carbon atoms) + (4 atoms of hydrogen per molecule)*(1.00797 grams per mole for hydrogen atoms) = 16.0429 grams per mole methane

In order to calculate the weight in grams of one mole of molecules of the compound, known as the isotopically averaged molecular mass, use the average atomic weight (in g/mol) of each of the elements in the molecular formula multiplied by the number of times each element is found in each molecule.

Chemical and atomic number interaction of atoms

Mass is concentrated in a nucleus, which is 1/10,000 the overall size of the atom, and contains neutrons and protons. Most of the volume of an atom is filled by the orbiting electrons. An atom's chemical interactions are determined by its cloud of electrons. The outermost electrons determine the basic chemical properties of the atom. Atoms with the same total number of electrons are said to be chemically "identical." Atoms attract or repel electrons until they have a balanced charge. The number of protons in the nucleus equals the number of electrons that are in a neutral atom. This also determines the chemical identity of the atom:

Number of protons = Atomic number

Quantum numbers

Schrödinger's model allowed for an electron to occupy a three-dimensional space. It is thus required that three coordinates, or quantum numbers, describe those orbitals in which electrons are found. The coordinates are the principal (n), angular (l), and magnetic (m) quantum numbers. These numbers describe size, shape and orientation in space of an atom's orbitals. The principal quantum number (n) describes the orbital's size. For example, those orbitals for which n = 2 are larger than those for which n = 1. The angular number (l), describes the shape of the orbital. Orbitals with spherical shapes are (l = 0), (l = 1) for polar, or (l = 2) for cloverleaf. The (m) describes the orbitals' orientation.

Stereochemistry

Stereochemistry is the branch of chemistry which studies and describes the three-dimensional spatial arrangement of atoms and molecules and is an extension of molecular geometry. It is particularly concerned with stereoisomers—versions of a given compound having the same chemical compositions but different configurations. Configuration is the arrangement of atoms in space, within a molecule, a variable having important effects in biological processes. Even a relatively simple molecule, such as a C tetrahedron bonded with four groups of atoms, has a large number of possible variations in configuration. The configuration of molecules has important effects on its reactivity and physical and biological processes. Thalidomide provides a dramatic example of the importance of isomers. One isomer of the drug prevents morning sickness while the other was found to cause birth defects. The only difference between the two versions is the molecular configuration.

Absolute configuration

Absolute configuration of a molecule is the exact position and orientation of its constituent atoms and groups of atoms. Because molecules are three dimensional, it is important for scientists to know "which way is up" when a given molecule is under consideration, especially in biological processes when the molecular configuration can have enormous consequences. As with nomenclature, standards have been developed which specify the positions of all atoms in the molecule. Absolute configuration can thus be discovered by comparing it to a reference compound whose configuration is known. Furthermore, it can be described by assigning each of the substituents atoms or groups a priority number based on atomic number; the lowest priority atom or group is then said to be "the bottom" of the molecule. Absolute configuration is foundational for biochemistry because certain organic molecules may only "fit" into biological receptors if they are the correct shape and configuration.

Models and lines for envisioning molecules

Atoms and molecules are complex three dimensional objects in motion. Although they and their bonding properties and structures can be represented with two dimensional drawings such as dot structures and structural formulas, the best models are those which represent the third dimension as well. Because this is difficult to do on two dimensional surfaces such as pages of a book, the following conventions represent three dimensions in molecular drawings:

- Solid lines represent chemical bonds on the plane of the page.
- Wedge-shaped lines represent bonds projecting forward out of the page.
- Dashed lines represent bonds projecting backward out of the page.

Three dimensionality can also be shown by pictures of ball-and-stick molecular

models and by "space-filling" models pictured as overlapping spheres.

Lewis dot structure

Lewis structures, also called Lewis electron dot formulas, are symbols in which an atom's valence electrons are represented as dots. The structures consist of the atom's periodic symbol surrounded by dots equaling the number of its valence electrons. Hydrogen has one valence electron, so its electron dot formula is H•, while Helium's is He: with its two valence electrons. Noble gases, with eight valence electrons, are represented with one pair of dots on each side of the element's symbol. They are useful for illustrating the transfer of electrons in reactions, particularly in those forming ionic compounds. They are also another way to represent the bonds and structure of simple molecules just as a structural formula would do.

Although the Lewis structure is a much simplified representation of the electron configuration of an atom, it is useful for thinking about molecular geometry. The dot structures predict the rough shape of the molecule through covalent bonds that will form by the location of their unpaired

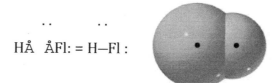

electrons. The example here shows the dot structures for H and Fl and the linear (the nuclei are aligned in a singular dimension) shape of an HF molecule. The unpaired valence electrons are represented by a single dot and are also the sites of the covalent bond joining the atoms. The bonded molecule is represented by the circular structures. The shape of a molecule can therefore be roughly predicted based on the number of valence electrons available in each atom.

Conformations

Structural formulas printed on a page make no attempt to illustrate the geometry or movement of a molecule. Molecules are moving, three dimensional structures and it is important to consider the rotational capabilities of the groups which make up a molecule. Groups bonded by single bonds are capable of spinning around the bond, much like a wheel spins around its axle. The different orientations in which a molecule may appear at any given time are its conformations. Conformations are not steady—one is always changing into another—and only give a view of a molecule as a "snapshot" of a moment in time. Conformations are different from isomers because the bond types and sequences do not change, only the orientation of the group at the end of the single bond.

Schrödinger equation

Austrian physicist Erwin Schrödinger proposed an equation describing the time dependence of quantum mechanical systems. It is a central factor in the theory of quantum mechanics and has been compared the Newton's second law in classical mechanics. Each system in the mathematical formulation of quantum mechanics is in concert with a complex Hilbert space, which is a generalization of Euclidean space and not restricted to finite dimensions, such that every instantaneous state of the system is described in that space by a unit vector. The vector encodes outcomes of all the possible measurements that are applied to the system. The vector becomes a function of time as the state of a system changes over a period of time. The equation is:

$$i\hbar\frac{\partial \Psi(\mathbf{r},\,t)}{\partial t} = \hat{H}\Psi(\mathbf{r},\,t)$$

In this, i is the unit imaginary number; $\hbar$ is Planck's constant divided by 2π, and the Hamiltonian H(t) is a self-adjoint operator that acts of the state space.

Aufbau principle

The Aufbau principle is a set of rules that help solve some of the modern atomic theory equations. Quantum numbers play a part in these rules. With each principal number n is an energy level called a shell. A shell 1 is n = 1, shell 2 is n = 2, etc. Each shell has subshells and can have more than one subshell. The number of subshells within a shell = n. Electrons reside in orbitals. The Aufbau principle says that the physical and chemical properties of elements are determined by the atomic structure. The principle rules for placing electrons within shells is known as the Aufbau principle. The rules are:

- The least energetically available subshell is where electrons are placed.
- At most, only two electrons can be held in an orbital.
- If two or more equal orbitals are available then these electrons should be dispersed before being paired.

Pauli exclusion principle

Wolfgang Pauli formulated the quantum mechanical principle which states that no two electrons within an atom may have quantum numbers that are identical. This also applies to fermions, which have half-integer spins. The building blocks of matter -- electrons, protons and neutrons -- are all subject to the Pauli exclusion principle. Many of the characteristic properties of matter, ranging from large-scale stability of matter to the existence of the periodic table of elements, are subject to the Pauli exclusion principle. These fermions have angular momentum and are considered antisymmetric states within quantum mechanics. Bosons are particles that are not fermions and have particles that use symmetric states in quantum theory. Bosons may only share quantum states and have integer spins such as the photon.

Planck's Constant

Planck's Constant can be shown by taking a rotating, charged conducting ball and slicing it perpendicular to its axis of rotation into tiny cylinders. Each of the cylinders will behave as a current loop.

What this means is that a rotating charged ball has a moment when it is magnetic. The electrons and protons are not rotating in conducting charged balls but are modeled as spinning charges; they also become magnetic Their momentum is angular, called "spin," and quantized in units of h. Planck's Constant = 6.626×10^{-34} J x s. In a magnetic field the electron or proton will have spins of only h/2 or -h/2, which are up or down depending on direction of the field.

Rutherford scattering

Ernest Rutherford concluded from the work of Geiger and Marsden that the majority of the mass was concentrated in a minute, positively charged region, or the nucleus, which was surrounded by electrons. When a positive alpha particle approached close enough to the nucleus it was strongly repelled; enough so that it had the ability to rebound at high angles. The small nucleus size explained the small amount of alpha particles that were repelled in this fashion. Rutherford scattering is also referred to as Coulomb scattering. This is because it relies on static electric, or Coulomb forces. The scattering led to development of the orbital theory of the atom, or what is known as the Bohr model. Rutherford was known as the "father of nuclear physics."

Bragg's law

W.H. and W.L Bragg, father and son, derived from experiments of X-ray diffraction of crystal surfaces at certain angles that real particles at the atomic scale existed. The experiments also provided a new way in which to study crystals in the form of X-ray diffraction. When an atom is hit by an X-ray, they make the electronic clouds move (as does other electromagnetic waves). This movement helps re-radiate waves with the same frequency, which is known as elastic or Rayleigh scattering. These re-emitted X-rays limit constructive or destructive interferences. The interference is constructive when a shift in phase is proportional to 2π. This expresses Bragg's law:

In this, n is an integer; λ is the X-ray wavelength; d is the spacing between the planes in the atomic lattice; and θ is the angle between the scattering planes and incident rays.

Bohr model

The Bohr model is a model of the atom that gives an explanation about matters such as line spectra. Neil Bohr postulated that the electrons which orbit an atom could only occupy certain orbits. Those were orbits in which angular momentum satisfied a particular equation:

$$L_n = mv_n r_n = nh / 2\pi \qquad (n = 1, 2, 3, ...)$$

Where m is the electron's mass, r is the radius of the orbit and v the orbital speed of the electron. Bohr proposed that the angular momentum of an electron is quantized. To analyze this, take the concept of circular motion and the potential energy of two charges. The electron has a charge of -e, while the nucleus has a charge of +Ze, where Z is the atomic number of the element. The energy is then:

$$\text{Energy of an electron} : E = KE + PE = 1/2 \, mv^2 - kZe^2 / r$$

The electron has uniform circular motion with the only force on the electron being an attraction between the negative electron and the positive nucleus. So: Rearrange the angular momentum equation to solve for velocity: Substituted in the nth level:

De Broglie waves

Louis de Broglie was a French physicist who introduced electron wave theory. This included the wave-particle duality theory of matter which assumes that light and matter can show properties of both waves and particles. His work led to the hypothesis:

"Any moving particle or object has an associated wave."

This created wave mechanics physics, which joined light and matter physics. De Broglie helped develop an explanation of wave mechanics that was unlike other models involving probability, which are dominant in quantum mechanics. This is called the de Broglie-Bohm theory after being improved by David Bohm. The interpretation by Bohm holds that the existence of a non-local universal wave function allows distant particles to instantly interact. The wave function grows according to Schrödinger's equation and directs the particle.

Davisson-Germer experiment

The Davisson-Germer experiment exhibits the wave nature of the electron

- 24 -

and confirmed de Broglie's earlier hypothesis. This helped give quantum mechanics a boost due to putting wave-particle duality on a stable experimental footing. Bragg's law for diffraction had been applied to the diffraction of X-rays, but this was the first application for particle waves. A vacuum apparatus was built by Davisson and Germer in order to measure the energies of electrons scattered from metal surfaces. Electrons from a heated filament were accelerated by voltage and allowed to strike the nickel metal's surface. The electron beam was aimed at the nickel which could be rotated to see angular dependence of the scattered electrons. The electron detector was mounted on an arc in order to rotate for observing electrons at different angles. They found a peak in the intensity of scattered electron beams at certain angles.

Copenhagen interpretation

The Copenhagen interpretation was formulated by Niels Bohr and Werner Heisenberg in Copenhagen circa 1927. It extended an earlier probabilistic interpretation that Max Born had proposed. The Copenhagen interpretation assumes that two processes influence the wave function. First is the unitary evolution based on the Schrödinger equation. The other is the process of the measurement. The first process can be interpreted that a wave function will have a wave function collapse in the second stage, or it can be imagined that the wave function serves as an alternate mathematical tool rather than a physical entity whose physical meaning is the ability for one to calculate the probabilities. Bohr said that only results of experiments should be predicted, thus more questions are philosophical rather than scientific.

Many-worlds interpretation

The many-worlds interpretation in quantum mechanics theory reject a non-deterministic and wave function collapse associated with the measurement in the Copenhagen interpretation. It favors a description along the lines of quantum entanglement -- where the quantum states of two or more objects are described as: referred to each other even though the objects are spatially separated -- and a reversible time of evolution of states. This is associated with measurement explained by the process of decoherence, in which a system interacts with its environment in a way that the different portions of its wave function may no longer interfere with each other. The many-worlds interpretations postulate that a state function for the universe obeying Schrödinger equation has no process of non-deterministic wave function collapse. Also theorized is that the universal state is a quantum superposition of perhaps infinite parallel universes.

Photoelectric effect

The photoelectric effect is a process in which light falling on a surface removes electrons from the surface. Einstein explained this effect and it was one of the earliest applications of quantum mechanics. To understand the effect, consider that light behaves like photons. Each electron is ejected by only one photon striking the surface. Quantum theory holds that frequency, f , of the light determines energy, E, of the photon in the light beam:

$$E = hf$$

where h is Planck's constant. The energy from the emitted electron is given by the photon's energy minus the energy that is required to release the electron from the surface. So, it depends on the light frequency that falls on the surface but not its intensity.

Double-slit experiment

The double-slit experiment lets light diffract through two slits and produce fringes on a screen. These fringes, or interference patterns, have light and dark regions that correspond to where light waves interfered constructively and destructively. The experiment may also be performed with a beam of atoms and electrons that show like interference patterns. This supports wave-particle duality predicted by quantum mechanics. But, a double-slit experiment may also be accomplished with water waves in a ripple tank. The explanation of the wave seen does not require quantum mechanics. Rather, the phenomenon is quantum mechanical only when quantum particles such as electrons, photons or electrons are manifested as waves.

Wheeler's delayed choice experiment

In 1983 John Archibald Wheeler proposed an experiment that was a variation of the double-slit experiment in which the target detector can be changed at the last moment through a delayed choice of the observer. There is a detector screen which detects the normal wave interference pattern producing the double slit which may be removed. Two tightly-focused telescopes are behind the screen and are pointed to see one slit or the other, detecting the path the photon traversed. If photons are observed with the screen, a wave-like behavior happens. If the photons are seen with the telescopes then particle-like behavior takes place. But there is another scenario, when the photon has originated from the other side of the universe and is bent by an intervening black hole so that it arrives by one or two different paths to the detector.

Quantum eraser experiment

The quantum eraser experiment is a double-slit experiment in which selective polarization and particle entanglement is used to determine into which slit a particle will go by measuring the particle's entangled partner. The partner never enters the experiment. The measurement of direction negates the interference pattern in the double-slit portion of the experiment. One can restore the interference pattern without changing anything in the double-slit experiment by destroying the directional information in the entangled particle that previously determined the path. This makes the experiment advantageous. The quantum eraser erases the directional information and restores interference without changing the double-slit experiment. The experiment can be modified, whether to measure or destroy the directional information; or can be delayed until after the entangled particle partner has/has not interfered with itself.

Quantum indeterminacy

Quantum indeterminacy is an apparent needed incompleteness in describing a physical system that is one of the characteristics of the quantum physics description. Before quantum physics, it was believed that a physical system with a determinate state specifically determines all the values of its properties that are measurable. Also prior to quantum physics, the values of its measurable properties were thought to uniquely determine the state. Quantum indeterminacy may be characterized by a probability distribution on the set of outcomes of measurements of an observable. The distribution is specifically determined by a system's state and quantum mechanics provides a way to calculate this probability distribution. This indeterminacy can be characterized quantitatively by a probability distribution on the set of outcomes of measurement of an observable, or a property that can be determined through a sequence of physical operations.

Tetraneutrons

A tetraneutron is a hypothetical cluster of four neutrons. This particle cluster is not supported by the present standard model of particle physics. But some empirical evidence suggesting this particle's existence exists based on an experiment by Francisco-Miguel Marques. The experiment used a method of watching the disintegration of beryllium and lithium nuclei using a particle accelerator to fire the atomic nuclei and produce a spray of particles from the collision. This is a potentially important discovery since nuclear theory suggests that the clusters should not be stable and therefore should not exist. Recent modifications have been made in experiments and if a bound tetraneutron can be confirmed it could significantly change the understanding of nuclear forces.

Weak interaction nuclear force

The weak interaction nuclear force is one of four fundamental forces of nature and is most commonly seen in beta decay and radioactivity. The word weak comes from the fact that the field strength is some 1013 times less strong than a nuclear force. This weak force affects all leptons and quarks and is the only force that affects neutrinos, a fermion. This weak interaction lets all quark and lepton particles and antiparticles interchange mass, energy, electric charge, and flavor (a quantum number of elementary particles related to their weak interactions effectively changing into one another). Their large mass is approximately 90 GeV/c2 and their mean life is only about 3 x 10-25 seconds by the uncertainty principle.

Standard Model of particle physics

The Standard Model is a theory developed in the 1970s describing strong, weak and electromagnetic forces as well fundamental particles that comprise matter. It is consistent with both special relativity and quantum mechanics. It is not a complete theory of fundamental interactions mainly because it does not give a description of gravitational force. The model contains both fermionic and bosonic particles. The fermions are basically particles of matter and bosons are transmission force particles. The theory holds that photons mediate electromagnetic interaction, W and Z bosons mediate weak nuclear force, eight gluon species mediate strong nuclear force, and Higgs bosons cause spontaneous symmetrical breaking of the electromagnetic and weak interaction gauge groups and are a reason for inertial mass to exist.

Cosmic rays

Cosmic rays are radiation that are made up of energetic particles that originate beyond the Earth but impinge on the Earth's atmosphere. Cosmic rays are mainly made of ionized nuclei, the majority of which are protons. Kinetic energy from cosmic ray particles span over 14 orders of magnitude with the flux of cosmic rays on the Earth's surface falling at about the inverse cube of the energy. A wide variety of particle energy reflects various sources. Cosmic rays start from processes on the Sun and extend to the farthest portions of the universe that is visible. They may have energies up to 1020 eV. Victor Hess, using electrometers to measure ion rates inside a sealed container, flew to 5,300 meters in a balloon in 1912 and found a four-fold increase in ionization over that at ground level. He explained it by assuming that great penetrating radiation enters the atmosphere.

Spallation

Spallation is the process in which heavy nuclei emit large numbers of nucleons due to being struck by high-energy protons, greatly reducing its atomic weight. Spallation takes place naturally in the Earth's atmosphere due to impacts of cosmic rays as well as on the surfaces of bodies in space, such as the moon and meteorites. Cosmic ray spallation is evidence that materials have been exposed on the surface of the body and, partly, gives a way to measure the length of time exposed. The composition of cosmic rays also indicate that they have undergone spallation before reaching the Earth (due to the proportion of such light elements as Li, B and Be which exceed the average cosmic abundances). The elements in cosmic rays were probably formed from oxygen, nitrogen, carbon, and maybe silicon from cosmic ray sources or during lengthy travel to Earth.

Electromagnetic radiation

Radiation is heat transferred by electromagnetic waves that are emitted and carry energy away from the object that omits them. Two bodies of heat do not need a medium for transferring heat in radiation such as is needed by convection and conduction. Instead, photons traveling at the speed of light act as the intermediaries. Heat transferred into or out of something has components that include emissivity, surface area, surface reflectivity temperature and geometric orientation. An object's emissivity and surface reflectivity are functions of both the composition and surface condition. Radiation as a means of transferring heat must account for thermal heat that is both incoming and outgoing.

Electromagnetic radiation is energy in the form of electromagnetic waves which consist of both a magnetic field component and an electrical field component. Electromagnetic waves travel at a velocity of 3.0×10^8 meters per second, the speed of light in a vacuum. There are various types of electromagnetic radiation which can differ from each other in wavelength and frequency. The wavelength and frequency are related by:

$$ v = \frac{c}{\lambda} $$

where c = speed of light; λ = wavelength; v = frequency.

Electromagnetic spectrum

The electromagnetic spectrum is the range of all possible radiation that is electromagnetic. The spectrum is also the range of electromagnetic radiation that is reflected, transmitted or emitted. The spectrum extends from the long-wavelength end, for frequencies used in power grids, to gamma radiation at the short wavelength end. It covers wavelengths from thousands of kilometers down to sizes that are fractional of atoms. Sunspots produce radiation every 22 years or a frequency of 1.4×10^{-9} Hz. Photons, at the other end, with arbitrarily high frequencies may be made by electrons colliding with positrons at appropriate energy. Photons of 1024 Hz can now be produced by man-made accelerators.

Types

Electromagnetic radiation differs in energy level and each type is spread over a range of wavelengths. The lowest energy level radiation is radio waves. These have the longest wavelengths ($\sim$1010 nm) and lowest frequency. The highest are gamma rays which have very short wavelengths ($\sim$ 10-3 nm) and high frequencies. The wavelength of the visible light region ranges from $\sim$ 400 nm (violet) to $\sim$ 700 nm (red). Between these two are the infrared spectrum, the UV spectrum, visible light and X-rays.

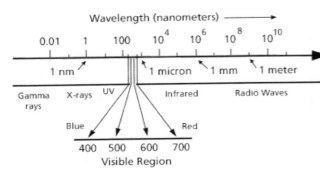

Electromagnetic Spectrum

Cherenkov radiation

Cherenkov radiation is electromagnetic radiation that is emitted when charged particles pass through insulators at speeds greater than that of light in the particular medium. The so-called "blue glow" that is known in nuclear reactors stems from Cherenkov radiation. It occurs because relativity holds that the speed of light in a vacuum is a universal constant (c), and the speed of light in a material may be much less than c. The speed of light in water is just 0.75c, for example. Cherenkov radiation occurs when charged particles, usually electrons, exceed the speed of light in an electrically insulated medium through which it travels. The intensity of Cherenkov radiation is in proportion to the velocity of the inciting particle and to the numbers of those particles. This radiation has higher frequencies and thus shorter wavelengths. Cherenkov radiation is used in detecting high-energy charged particles.

Thermal radiation

Thermal radiation is electromagnetic radiation from objects that are caused by its temperature. It has rapid increases in power and frequency along with increased temperature. Radiant heat is used in homes, such as when electricity is forced through materials for conductive heating. Black bodies are objects that take in all electromagnetic radiation falling on it. Heat radiators are used, such as those mounted on the interior surface of payload bay doors in the Space Shuttle. The shuttle can orbit and still allow the radiators to work. These radiators are used as black body radiators, but the coatings appear white to the eye because of the need to reflect wavelengths that are visible in order to avoid their absorption.

Electromagnetic wave equation

The electromagnetic wave equation is a second-order partial differential equation that guides the propagation of electromagnetic waves through a medium or in a vacuum. The equation written in terms of either the electric field, E, or the magnetic field, H, is such that:

$$\nabla^2 \mathbf{E} - \frac{1}{c^2}\frac{\partial^2 \mathbf{E}}{\partial t^2} = 0$$

$$\nabla^2 \mathbf{H} - \frac{1}{c^2}\frac{\partial^2 \mathbf{H}}{\partial t^2} = 0$$

where c is the speed of light in the medium. In a vacuum, c = 2.998 x 108 meters per second which is the speed of light in free space. The electromagnetic wave equation is derived from Maxwell's equations. In a linear isotropic, not-dispersive medium, the magnetic flux density, B, relates to the magnetic field, H, by:

$$B = o\mu H$$

where ημ is the magnetic permeability of the medium; B is normally called the magnetic field in most modern literature and H is the "H vector" or auxiliary magnetic field.

Hazards

Electromagnetic radiation can be either ionizing radiation or non-ionizing radiation depending on whether it is able to ionize atoms and break chemical bonds. Frequencies such as ultraviolet and higher, such as gamma rays or X-rays, are ionizing. These have their own potential dangers. Non-ionizing radiation is not capable of having such effects on molecules, at least in this context. Three potential hazards that are considered major exist with non-ionizing electromagnetic radiation. They are electrical, biological and fire. The induced current caused by radiation also can pose significant dangers in handling pyrotechnics. Induced current can cause electric shock to humans or animals. A strong electromagnetic field may cause electric currents which flow over air gaps to the ground, causing sparks and fire. The biological hazard stems from electromagnetic fields causing dielectric heating and can lead to tissue and other bodily damage.

Infrared radiation

Infrared radiation is a form of electromagnetic radiation with a wavelength longer than visible light but shorter than microwave radiation. The name stems from the Latin "infra," meaning below and red because it is the color of visible light of longest wavelength. Three orders of magnitude are spanned by infrared radiation and it has wavelengths that are from 750 nm to 1 mm. Infrared has divided regions: near infrared, defined by water absorption and used commonly in fiber optic telecommunications because of low losses in the glass medium; short wavelength or short wave, in which water absorption significantly increases at 1,450 nm; mid wavelength; long wavelength and far infrared.

Night-vision equipment: Night-vision equipment such as that used by military, police and firefighters uses infrared radiation when not enough visible light is available to see an object. Radiation is detected and turned into an image on a screen. Objects with higher temperatures show up in different shades than cooler objects which allows police and military to find important thermal targets such as humans and battle tanks. Infrared radiation is not heat itself but rather another effect of heat. Thermal detectors do not find heat directly but instead find the difference in the infrared radiation of objects. Certain materials emit more or less infrared radiation upon increase or decrease of temperature, although it depends on the materials' composition. Firefighters use infrared imaging in smoke-filled spaces because smoke is more transparent to infrared than it is to visible light.

Radioactive decay

Radioactive decay is a set of processes that allow unstable atomic nuclei, or nuclides, to emit subatomic particles, or radiation. The decay is a random process and it is not possible to predict an individual atom's decay. The becquerel, Bq, is the SI unit for measuring radioactive decay. One Bq is defined as one decay event per second. Certain interactions of protons including strong nuclear force, weak nuclear force and electrostatic force play a part in decay. Some particle configurations in a nucleus have properties that if they were to shift slightly those particles could be considered a lower-energy structure. A decay event needs activation energy. Quantum mechanical particles continuously and randomly move. So, if constituent particles move together, the nucleus can destabilize spontaneously.

Half-life of a radioactive isotope

The half-life of a radioactive isotope is the time required for one half of the original atoms in a sample to decay. It is the principal characteristic used to distinguish one radioactive substance from another and can vary greatly from nucleus to nucleus. A quantity is said to subject to exponential decay if a decrease occurs at a rate that is proportional to its value. All radioactive decays obey first-order kinetics. Those quantities subject to exponential decay are known by the symbol N. If the quantity is denoted by N, the value of N at a particular time t is expressed by:

$$\frac{dN}{dt} = -\lambda N.$$

The solution is:

$$N = Ce^{-\lambda t}.$$

This is the form of the equation most commonly used to describe exponential decay. The constant of integration C is often written N0 since it stands for the original quantity.

Alpha decay

Alpha decay is a type of radioactive decay in which an alpha particle is ejected from an atomic nucleus through the electromagnetic force and results in a nucleus with a mass number 4 less and an atomic number 2 less. An example:

$$^{238}U \rightarrow {}^{234}Th + \alpha.$$

The alpha particle is a helium nucleus, both atomic number and mass number are conserved. Alpha decay can be looked at as nuclear fission, in which the parent nucleus splits into a pair of daughter nuclei. Alpha decay is governed by the strong nuclear force, or the force between two or more nucleons. Alpha particles have speeds of 15,000 km/s when a typical kinetic energy of 5 Me V.

Beta decay

Beta decay is radioactive decay in which there is an emission of a beta particle, a high-energy electron or positron. In electron emission it is known as beta minus (β-). In positron emission it is known as beta plus (β+). In β- decay there is conversion of a neutron into a proton caused by the interaction of the electron is emitted with an anti-neutrino. This is because of the conversion of a down quark (first-generation quark with a charge of 1/3e) to an up quark (a first-generation quark with a charge of +(2/3)e by a W boson emission. In β+ decay, a proton is converted into a neutron, a positron and a neutrino:

$$\text{energy} + p^+ \rightarrow n^0 + e^+ + \nu_e$$

Double beta decay

In double beta decay, unstable nuclei decay by the conversion of a neutron in the nucleus to a proton and emitting an electron and anti-neutrino. Beta decay must have a greater binding energy than the original nucleus. With some nuclei such as germanium-76, the nuclei, with an atomic number of one higher, has a smaller binding energy that prevents beta decay from happening. With germanium-76, the nuclei with an atomic number two higher, selenium-76, has greater binding energy so the process of "double beta" decay can take place. In double beta decay, two neutrons in the nuclei convert to protons and two electrons and two anti-neutrinos are omitted. It is the rarest type of radioactive decay that is known.

Neutrinoless double beta decay

Double beta decay is also called two neutrino double beta decay since two neutrinos or anti-neutrinos are emitted. If the neutrino is a Majorina particle in which the anti-neutrino and the neutrino are one and the same particle, then a neutrinoless double beta decay could possibly take place. When neutrinoless double beta decay occurs, the emitted neutrino is quickly absorbed as its anti-

particle by another nucleon of the nucleus. So, the total kinetic energy of the two electrons are exactly the difference in binding energy that is between the initial and final nuclei states. Experiments to look for neutrinoless double beta decay have taken place or have been proposed. Such a discovery would indicate that neutrinos are Majorana particles which allow a neutrino mass calculation.

Gamma rays

A gamma ray (γ) is electromagnetic radiation that is produced from radioactive decay or other nuclear processes such as an electron annihilation, in which an electron and positron collide. No physical difference exists between X-rays and gamma rays that have the same energy, they are set apart by their origin. Gamma ray describes high-energy electromagnetic radiation by nuclear transitions while X-rays are high-energy radiation caused by energy transitions from electrons that are accelerating. Gamma rays penetrate more than either alpha or beta radiation, both of which are not electromagnetic radiation, but is not as ionizing. Gamma sources have a wide variety of uses ranging from medicine to industry.

Spontaneous fission

Spontaneous fission, or SF, is a form of radioactive decay that is typical of very heavy isotopes. This fission is possible, in theory, for any atomic nucleus with a mass greater than or equal to 100 amu. In reality, however, spontaneous fission is only energetically possible for atomic masses above 230 amu. Most susceptible to spontaneous fission are those trans-actinide elements such as rutherfordium. Spontaneous decay by fission does happen for uranium and thorium but it is not observed for the majority of radioactive breakdowns. The mathematical formula for spontaneous fission occurring is:

$$Z^2/A \approx 45.$$

Spontaneous fission goes through the same process as nuclear fission only it does not generate a neutron flux necessary for going "critical" and continuing such functions. The other distinction between spontaneous and nuclear fission is the former is not self-sustaining.

Isomeric transition

Isomeric transition, a radioactive decay process, happens in an atom when its nucleus is in an excited meta-state, such as after the emission of alpha or beta particles. The nucleus has extra energy released by gamma ray emission that returns the nucleus to the ground state. Gamma emission is similar, but it involves excited meta-states. After decay, the nucleus remains in an excited state. When energy is released as gamma rays there is no change in Z or A = isomeric. Gamma rays may transfer energy directly to tightly-bound electrons that cause ejection from an atom in a process called internal conversion.

Internal conversion

Internal conversion is a radioactive decay process where gamma rays emitted from a nucleus are photoelectrically absorbed by one of the most tightly bound electrons. This causes it to be ejected from the atom. Following ejection of the internal conversion electron, another shell electron fills the vacancy along with a corresponding emission of one or more X-rays or an auger electron, the latter of which produced by an auger emission in which an electron of an atom causes the emission of a second electron; this second electron ejected is the Auger electron. Favorable circumstances for internal conversion are when energy gaps between nuclear levels are small; this is the only way for de-excitations of 0+->0+ transitions can occur.

Electron capture

Electron capture, a decay mode for isotopes, occurs when too many protons are in the nucleus of an atom and there is not sufficient energy to emit a positron. This will continue to be an able decay mode for radioactive isotopes that can decay by positron emission. If the difference in energy between the parent and daughter atom is less than 1.022 MeV, positron emission cannot happen and electron capture is the only mode of decay. One example is Rubidium-83 decaying to Krypton-83, which can only happen by electron capture. In such a case, one of the electron's orbitals (normally from the K or L electron shells) is captured by a proton in the nucleus and forms a neutron and a neutrino.

Nuclear reaction

A nuclear reaction is a process in which two nuclear particles or nuclei collide, producing different products than the original. A reaction can encompass more than two colliding particles but such events are very rare. If particles collide and separate without undergoing change, the process is termed a collision instead of a reaction. It can be written with an equation in which each particle in the reaction is written with its chemical symbol then atomic number subscripted as well as a superscripted atomic mass. Neutron is n, electron e, and the proton may be represented by H or p. The sum of the atomic numbers must be on each side of the equation in order to be balanced; the sum of the atomic masses must also be on each side and are also equal. Such as:

$$^6_3Li + ^2_1H \rightarrow ^4_2He + ?$$

The balanced equation for the helium nucleus is:

$$^6_3Li + ^2_1H \rightarrow ^4_2He$$

Release of energy

Energy in a reaction can be calculated according to a reference table of very accurate particle masses. For instance, the reference tables indicate that the ^6_3Li nucleus has an atomic weight of 6.015 amu, the deuteron is 2.014 amu and the nucleus is 4.0026 amu. So, the left side total mass is 6.015 + 2.014 = 8.029; right side total mass is 2 x 4.0026 = 8.0052; the missing mass is 8.029 - 8.0052 = 0.0238

amu. The mass that is missing stems from energy that is released from the reaction. It's source is the binding nuclear energy. To determine how much energy has been released, Einstein's E=mc2 can be used. One amu = 931 MeV, so energy released is 0.0238 x 931 MeV = 22.4 MeV.

Neutron radiation

Neutron radiation consists of free neutrons. The neutrons may come during nuclear fission, nuclear fusion or from very high energy reactions as well as other sources. Neutron radiation is often called indirectly ionizing radiation. It ionizes atoms differently than neutrons having no charge. But interactions are largely ionizing such as when neutron absorption causes gamma emission and the gamma rays remove electrons from an atom or a nucleus recoils from neutron interaction and is ionized, causing more traditional ionization in other atoms. Neutrons are more penetrating than alpha or beta radiation because they are not charged and they sometimes penetrate more than gamma radiation. Neutron radiation has the ability to induce radioactivity in most substances it touches including body tissues of humans. This happens through neutrons captured by atomic nuclei and transformed in radionuclide. This process is the basis for much of the radioactive material from detonated nuclear weapons.

Classes of nuclear reactors

Nuclear chain reactions are started, controlled and sustained at a steady rate in a nuclear reactor. This is opposed to a nuclear explosion in which chain reactions occur in a split second. Reactors have many uses, the major one being electric power generation and sometimes for producing plutonium to be used in nuclear weapons. All commercial reactors in the U.S. operate on nuclear fission. Reactors are generally divided into two classes: thermal reactors using slow or thermal neutrons and fast reactors that use neutrons to sustain the fission chain reaction and are characterized by a lack of material for moderating. Thermal reactors have moderating materials which are meant to slow the neutrons until they approach the average kinetic energy of surrounding particles, in other words until they are thermalized. They need highly enriched, sometimes weapons grade, fuel or plutonium so a reduction can occur in the amount of U-238 that would otherwise capture fast neutrons.

Nuclear meltdown

A nuclear meltdown happens whenever nuclear reactor cores melt. It usually is thought of as a serious nuclear accident. The reactor core may melt through the reactor floor chamber and drop down, continuing downward until it melts so that surrounding material dilutes and cools to a temperature that is no longer hot enough to cause melting through the material underneath, or until it hits groundwater. A thermonuclear explosion does not happen in meltdowns, but a steam explosion can happen if water is hit. Geometry and water is important in maintaining the chain reaction so the molten core cannot form uncontrolled critical mass. Molten reactor cores continue generating heat that is sufficient through radioactive decay so that it maintains or even increases water temperature.

Light water nuclear reactors

Nuclear fission reactors that are used for electric power generation are considered "light water reactors." Light water, which is ordinary water, is used as the moderator in American reactors. The water is also used as a cooling agent and the heat is taken away to make steam for moving turbines in electric generators. Ordinary water use requires a certain amount of uranium fuel enrichment before the criticality of the reactor is maintained. Two types of light water reactors exist. Pressurized water reactors are those in which water passes over the reactor core as a moderator and coolant does not flow to the turbine but is instead kept in a pressurized loop. Water passes over the reactor core in a boiling water reactor in order to act as moderator and coolant also acts as the source of steam for the turbine.

Fast breeder reactors

Neutrons given off by fission reaction can, under certain circumstances, breed more fuel from isotopes than would otherwise be non-fissionable. Plutonium-239 is the most common breeding reaction from non-fissionable uranium-238. Uranium-238 is bombarded with neutrons that set off two successive beta decays with plutonium production. How much plutonium is made is dependent on the breeding ratio. Fast breeder relates to the configuration types which actually produce more fissionable fuel than they use. An example is a liquid metal fast-breeder reactor. The reason for this is because non-fissionable uranium-238 is some 140 time more abundant than fissionable U-235 and can be converted efficiently into Pu-239 by neutrons from a fission chain reaction.

Organic Chemistry

Chemical reactions

The classic chemical reaction is a transfer of electrons resulting in a transformation of the substances involved in the reaction. The changes may be in composition or configuration of a compound or substance, and result in one or more products being generated which were not present in isolation before the reaction occurred. For instance, when oxygen reacts with methane (CH_4), water and carbon dioxide are the products; one set of substances ($CH_4 + O$) was transformed into a new set of substances ($CO_2 + H_2O$). Reactions are classified in many ways, some of which are as follows: as combination or synthesis, in which two or more compounds unite to form a more complex compound; decomposition, in which a compound is broken down into its constituent compounds or elements; and isomerization, in which compounds undergo structural changes without changing their atomic composition.

Some of the different types of chemical reactions are described below:
- Combination reactions: when pairs of reactants combine to produce a single substance. The reactions take place when it the energy is favorable to do so. For instance:
  - C(s) + O2(g) -> CO2(g)
  - N2(g) + 3H2(g) -> 2NH3(g)
  - CaO(s) + H2O(1) -> Ca(OH)2(s)
- Decomposition: refers to the reaction involving those molecules which are stable at room temperature and decompose when heated:
  - 2KC1O3(s)->2KC1(s) + 3O3(g)
  - PbCO3(s)->2PbO(s) +CO2(g)
- Single substitution: when a reaction involves an element that displaces another in a compound such as when a copper strip displaces silver atoms and produces copper nitrate and precipitating silver crystals of metal:
  - Cu(s) + 2AgNO3(aq) -> 2Ag(s) + Cu(NO3)2(aq)
- Double substitution: when a reaction looks as if it is exchanging parts of the reactants. An example:
  - 2KI(aq) + Pb(NO3)2(aq) -> 2KNO3 (aq) + PbI(s)

Types

Electron transfer, or redox reactions, occurs when electrons move from one atom to another, changing the charge of the ion. Because the charge has changed, the oxidation number also changes. Oxidation is an important class of redox reactions in which the oxidation number increases. Commonly, any reaction in which oxygen combines with other substances is oxidation. Rusting iron and burning wood are both examples of oxidation. Precipitation, or ion combination reactions, occurs when positive and negative compounds in solution combine to form an insoluble ionic compound. Acid-base reactions occur when an acid reacts with a base and an ion of hydrogen transfers to the base. Polymerization reactions occur when simple molecules, also called monomers, combine to form complex molecules, or polymers.

Mechanisms

Chemical reactions normally occur when electrons are transferred from one atom or molecule to another. Reactions and reactivity depend on the octet rule, which describes the tendency of atoms to gain or lose electrons until their outer energy levels contain eight. Reactions always result in a change in composition or constitution of a compound. They depend on the presence of a reactant, or substance undergoing change, a reagent, or partner in the reaction less transformed than the reactant (such as a catalyst), and products, or the final result of the reaction. Reaction conditions, or environmental factors, are also important components in reactions. These include conditions such as temperature, pressure, concentration, whether the reaction occurs in solution, the type of solution, and presence or absence of catalysts. Reactions are described with the following equation:
Reagent(s)
Reactant(s)Product(s)
Reaction
conditions

Reactions

Classes
Organic chemistry and biochemistry are the study of large numbers of compounds involved in complex reactions. These classes of reactions consist of broad categories containing many subsets.

- Addition reactions are the combination of two reactants into a single, more complex product. Atoms are added to adjacent atoms forming a new compound.
- Elimination reactions occur when a single compound is split into two smaller compounds, one of which is usually a simple molecule such as H_2O or HCl. Atoms are eliminated from the original compound and usually bond to adjacent C atoms in the reactant(s).
- In Hydrolysis reactions a large molecule reacts with water and is split into two smaller molecules. These are the reactions which change starch into glucose for metabolism.
- Hydrogenation reactions occur when gaseous H combines with hydrocarbons and produces a saturated compound—a compound in which the C atoms are bonded to the maximum possible number of H atoms.

Alkanes and cycloalkanes
Alkanes are a class of saturated hydrocarbons which have formed themselves into long chains. Cycloalkanes are saturated hydrocarbons in the shape

of rings. A Greek prefix before the name indicates the number of C atoms in the alkane; e.g. heptane contains seven C atoms. Because alkanes and cycloalkanes are highly stable, they are not very reactive because electrons are held in small orbits around the C and H atoms, making them less available for reactions. They can react under extreme conditions with substantial reaction energy to get them started. These reactions are generally classified into two groups: combustion, which is the often explosive reaction of alkanes with O, and halogenation, in which a halogen atom (from Group 17 on the periodic table) takes the place of an H atom in the presence of light.

Alkanes are less dense than water, which explains why gasoline, which is largely a collection of alkanes, floats on water. The molecules are nonpolar and are not soluble in water, which is polar. Their nonpolarity makes alkanes solvents of other nonpolar organic substances such as fats and oils following the "like dissolves like" rule of solubility. The boiling point of alkanes increases with increasing complexity and molecular weight. For example, methane, a simple, unbranched alkane boils at −164° C, while decane, a complex branched alkane boils at 174.1° C. Cycloalkanes are similar in physical properties in the predictability of density and boiling points. The higher the molecular weight of alkanes and cycloalkanes, the higher their respective density and boiling point.

Homologous series: A homologous series is a group of organic compounds sharing the same general formula, the same functional groups (and thus similar physical properties), and which differ predictably and incrementally as their relative size and atomic mass change. The most dramatic examples of a homologous series are the alkanes (methane, ethane, propane, butane, pentane, and so on). Each successive alkane differs from its predecessor in the presence of one additional CH_2 group, so the alkane's size and molecular mass increase accordingly. Alkenes and alkynes also appear in homologous series and exhibit the same periodic trends based on predictable changes at each successive step. It is important to remember that homologous series, while having exactly the same composition and proportions of constituent chemicals, may appear in many different isomers and thus have very different properties.

Alkenes

Alkenes are hydrocarbons structurally related to alkanes. They are characterized by C=C double bonds, making them unsaturated, and are very common in nature. Reactions associated with them typically involve the addition of functional groups or elements to the –ene parent hydrocarbon. One important reaction of this type is called hydrogenation because hydrogen gas combines with the alkene. The double C=C bonds are broken resulting in the formation of a saturated alkane. This process is also called alkene reduction because the double bonds are reduced to single bonds. This reaction has a high activation energy, and therefore is a slow reaction. Several catalysts have been synthesized which will speed up these reactions. In biological reactions such as those occurring in cells, hydrogenation or reduction of alkenes occurs with the aid of complex enzymes which serve as catalysts and sources of H.

Alcohols

Alcohols are a functional group containing oxygen and hydrogen (—OH, also called a hydroxyl group) bonded to the parent hydrocarbon with a single bond. An alcohol has multiple sites of reaction and different reaction types in which specific bonds are broken. In acid-base reactions, the O—H bond is broken. Depending on conditions, alcohols can act as acids or bases because they can be proton donors or acceptors. The C—O bond breaks in substitution reactions in which the hydroxyl group is replaced by something else. The C—O bond and C—H bond of an adjacent C atom are broken in elimination reactions in which a single molecule splits to form two products. The O—H and C—H bonds of the hydroxyl bearing atom are broken in oxidation reactions in which oxygen combines with C in place of H atoms.

An alkoxy (or alkoxyl) group is any group and an oxygen atom attached to an ether. It can react with hydrogen to form an alcohol.

Dehydration is a very important reaction involving alcohols in which H and O atoms are removed as H_2O. It is an elimination reaction because two or more covalent bonds are broken in a single alcohol molecule and a C=C bond is formed in the product, forming an alkene. If two or more alcohol molecules are involved in the dehydration reaction, an ether is the product.

Ethanol (CH_3CH_2OH) is the alcohol in alcoholic beverages and is a product of fermentation. Other substances are sometimes added to ethanol to make it unfit for drinking; such altered ethanol is called denatured alcohol.

Primary, secondary, and tertiary alcohols are those in which the alkoxy group (–OH) is bonded to the primary, secondary, or tertiary C atoms, respectively.

Aldehydes and ketones

Aldehydes are carbonyl groups (C=O) to which at least one hydrogen atom is attached. Formaldehyde is the simplest known aldehyde, with two H atoms attached to the C (COH_2). Ketones occur when a carbonyl C atom is bonded to two other C atoms, which are often parts of long hydrocarbon structures such as alkanes or cycloalkanes. Aldehydes and ketones are common classes of chemicals, especially in non-biological organic molecules. In common names, suffixes identify the compounds as aldehydes (-al) or ketones (-one), such as ionone, an aromatic compound found in irises and perfumes. Common reactions include reduction reactions, in which both aldehydes and ketones can be reduced to alcohols by breaking the C=O double bonds and adding H. By contrast, aldehydes engage easily in oxidation

- 41 -

reactions, as in the addition of O- , to form carboxylic acid; ketones are not easily oxidized.

Acetal is a product of an aldehyde's reaction with an alcohol and is an important compound in carbohydrate chemistry.

Hemiacetals are unstable intermediates on their way to becoming acetals; their transformation is completed in the presence of an acid catalyst.

Benedict's reagent is an important component of experiments involving aldehydes. It is a solution with mild oxidizing properties containing Cu^{2+} ions and produces a red precipitate in the presence of aldehydes.

Ketals are products of a ketone's reaction with alcohol. Hemiketals are the intermediates in such reactions and are very unstable.

Tollen's reagent is used for similar purposes but contains silver ions instead of copper. In the presence of aldehydes, the silver in solution precipitates to form solid silver.

Carboxylic acids

Carboxylic acids are compounds formed when a carboxyl group (CO_2H) bonds to a hydrocarbon unit such as an alkane or alkene. Formic, acetic, and stearic acids are common carboxylic acids. In decarboxylation of these compounds, a substitution reaction, the carboxyl group is replaced by a hydrogen atom. These

reactions are important in biological processes. These acids may also be converted to anhydrides (compounds without water) by reactions, usually at high temperature, which break the bonds in the carboxyl group and produce H_2O. Cleaving the C=O bond and removing the OH group from the carboxyl results in an acyl with double or triple bonds between the C and remaining O. These groups react quickly with halides to form compounds such as acyl chloride (OCCl).

:O:

σ

—C—O—H

Carboxyl

Benzenes

Benzene (C_6H_6) is an important cyclic organic compound. The electrons of its C atoms are delocalized resulting in combinations of single and double bonds, a structure which gives benzenes unusual stability. Compounds with strong, usually pleasant odors are often attached to benzene parents, so early chemists named these compounds aromatic compounds. Many benzene compounds have no odor, however. Common reactions include the following:

Aromatic electrophilic substitution: the most important class of reactions associated with benzene. In these reactions one H atom of the benzene is replaced by an electrophile which can be an atom or, more often, a molecule or functional group. This class contains subclasses of reactions such as halogenation (benzene + a halogen), nitration (benzene + a nitrate), sulfonation (benzene + a sulfate), alkylation, and acylation.

Amines and amides

Amines ($R—NH_2$) are a functional group containing nitrogen which form compounds vital to biological processes. They form when a hydrogen from an ammonia molecule (NH_3) is replaced by an organic compound. They can be primary, secondary, or tertiary amines, depending on how many atoms are bonded to the N atom. Amines react with acyl chlorides ($Cl—C=O$) and acid anhydrides in nucleophilic substitution, producing amides. They neutralize carboxylic acid in an acid-base reaction to produce ammonium carboxylate. Tertiary amines react with strong halogen acids to form ammonium salts. Amides ($O=C—N$) are another functional group; the most important of their reactions is hydrolysis in which the addition of water severs the C—N bond to create amine and carboxylic acid.

Esters

Esters ($O=C—O$) are a functional group often derived from carboxylic acids from which a H atom has been removed. This process is usually a condensation reaction in which two hydrogen-containing groups or compounds react, joining their H and releasing it as water. Such condensation reactions that produce an ester are called esterification reactions. The most important class of reactions associated with esters is hydrolysis, a reaction in which the ester is broken down by water to yield an alcohol and a carboxylic acid or salt. Hydrolysis of esters may be catalyzed by an acid or a base; if the catalyst is a base, the process if called saponification. Esters may also form amides through a reaction with primary or secondary amines at high temperatures.

Ethers

Ethers are a functional group containing an O atom bonded to two alkyl groups. "Ethers" is also the name of the class of chemicals containing an ether group. They are somewhat soluble in water because the O bonds readily with H and they have a relatively low boiling point. Ethers can be derived from the dehydration of alcohols through heat and a hydrogen-rich catalyst. Nucleophilic displacement of alkyl halides also yields ethers. Ethers are not very reactive in the pure state, but their substituents groups can be highly combustible, as with diethyl ether. Hydrolysis breaks ethers down, but only under drastic conditions such as boiling in the presence of strong halogen acids. Ethers form explosive peroxides in reactions with adjacent CH groups.

Acyl halides

An acyl halide is a compound derived from either a hydrogen acid or a carboxylic acid in which a hydroxyl group (–OH) has been replaced by a halogen. A double bond forms between C and O with two single bonds joining the C with the halogen atom and a root molecule. Acyl halides are synthetic molecules and are most often used as intermediates in reactions to form other compounds. In hydrolysis reactions, they form carboxylic acid and a hydrogen halide. They are useful in forming esters through a substitution reaction with alcohol and amides by reacting with amines. They also react with benzene (aromatic) rings to form an aromatic ketone using a strong acid catalyst. Acyl halides are quite reactive and somewhat toxic.

Enantioselectivity, regioselectivity, and diastereoselectivity

Reactions in which a certain type of product is preferred, though various isomers are equally possible, are called selective reactions. A prefix before selective identifies the type of isomer predominately formed in such selective reactions. Enantioselectivity refers to the tendency of a reaction to form a specific enantiomer (nonsuperimposable stereoisomer). Regioselectivity is the same principle applied to "regions" of the molecule; some reactions produce more compounds with a specific orientation of appended groups than isomers with different orientations. Diastereomers are isomers which are not mirror images of each other and can exhibit different properties and reactivity. Diastereoselectivity describes reactions in which one stereoisomer is preferred over another as product; the reaction produces more of the favored variety.

Metabolic pathways

Metabolism refers to an organism's ability, through chemical reactions, to produce and/or consume energy. Metabolic pathways are complex series of reactions in living cells which enable the biological processes. The pathways are highly complex, but well ordered and predictable, consisting of a series of chemical reactions designed either for catabolism—the breakdown of biomolecules, usually to produce energy, or anabolism—the synthesis of biomolecules. Photosynthesis is a widely known metabolic pathway which allows green plants to use energy from sunlight, water, and nutrients to produce the energy they need to live and grow. The processes commonly referred to as digestion, by which the human body extracts energy from food, is a series of enormous metabolic pathways. Because the chemical reactions involved are often not species-specific, understanding a metabolic pathway on a molecular and chemical level applies to other organisms that use the same process.

Factors influencing reactivity

In addition to describing the tendency of a substance to react, reactivity also refers to the speed with which reactions take place. Several factors influence this aspect of reactivity, including the purity of a compound or the presence of contaminants, the surface area of a substance, and the crystal structure of a substance that is in a solid state. An element's electron configuration is also an important factor because atoms "want" to reach their most stable possible configuration, so they react with other atoms in order to achieve this. Atoms with single, unpaired electrons, such as H, react quickly with other elements to achieve a more stable configuration - such

- 44 -

as the formation of diatomic hydrogen, in which the orbital is filled to its capacity.

Photosynthesis

Photosynthesis is the process, in plants, of capturing light energy and using it to convert carbon dioxide and water into sugars. Its generalized formula is:

$$6 \, CO_2 + 6 \, H_2O + light \rightarrow C_6H_{12}O_6 + 6O_2$$
$$(keq=10-500)$$

Photosynthesis is a light-driven, oxidation-reduction reaction. This is known as a "redox reaction." Redox reactions involve the stable transfer of electrons between atoms. The primary molecule that is responsible for catching light energy for the photosynthesis process is chlorophyll. Chlorophyll makes a transition to a higher state of energy when it absorbs a photo of light:

$$chl + a \, photon \rightarrow chl*$$

The energy can be dissipated as fluorescence, heat, resonance transfer or redox reaction.

Laboratory-induced chemical synthesis

Chemical synthesis is the intended use of chemical reactions to produce a product or products. This may take place by using manipulations that are physical and chemical. It usually involves one or more reaction. In laboratory usage, this implies the process can be reproduced, will be reliable and can be established to take place in other laboratories. The synthesis starts by selecting a compound that is a reactant. Various types of reactions may be applied in order to synthesize a product or a product that is intermediate. Reaction yield refers to the amount of product a chemical synthesis makes. Yields are usually expressed in mass as grams or as a percentage of a theoretical quantity of a product that might be produced. Types of synthesis include total synthesis, organic synthesis and telescopic synthesis.

Chemical synthesis as a chemical reaction

Chemical synthesis can also define a somewhat narrow and restricted type of specific chemical reaction that is a direct combination reaction in which two or more reactants combine and form a single product. The form for this reaction is: A + B -> AB where A and B are elements or compounds, and AB is also a compound containing A and B. An example is the formation of table salt:

$$2Na + Cl_2 \rightarrow 2 \, NaCl$$

There are four special synthesis rules:

- Metal-oxide + H_2O -> metal (OH)
- Nonmetal oxide + H_2O -> oxi-acid
- Metal chloride + O_2 -> metal chloride
- Metal-oxide + CO_2 -> metal (CO_3)

Energy

Energy is required for chemical reactions to occur and is released during reactions. One way to think of reactions is the breaking and formation of chemical bonds. Because chemical bonds have measurable strength, they tend to stay together unless acted upon by an external force, or energy; this energy is the reaction's activation energy. When bonds are broken or formed, energy stored in the bonds or substances is released. Energy on both sides of reactions occurs in various forms such as kinetic energy, heat, and light, and its measurement is an important part of understanding and balancing reactions and equations. Measuring the energy of reactants compared to that of products yields a difference in energy, or enthalpy, symbolized in equations by $\Delta H°$, which may be thought of as the "heat" of a reaction (though energy does not always take the form of heat).

Exothermic, endothermic, activation energy, and reaction equilibrium

Exothermic reactions are chemical reactions in which energy is released or produced, such as in combustion. In endothermic reactions, external energy is required for the reaction to occur and is absorbed from the surroundings. Some reactions require energy to start the reaction, this energy is called activation energy. A match applied to tissue paper is an example of activation energy. When the same number of atoms is present on the reactant side of an equation as on the product side, the reaction is said to be in equilibrium. All atoms of a substance must be accounted for after it undergoes a chemical reaction. For instance, methane reacting with oxygen produces water and carbon dioxide, but all atoms in the original substances are still present, albeit in different combinations.

Dynamic equilibrium

Dynamic equilibrium is a form of chemical equilibrium as applied to solutions. Solutes and solvents continually move around in solution and some particles of the solute reattach and take on their original forms; they "drop out" of solution. This process is called crystallization and is the opposite of dissolution. When the rates of dissolution and crystallization are equal, a solution is said to have achieved dynamic equilibrium. All solutions will eventually reach dynamic equilibrium unless they are subject to external energy, such as an increase in temperature or agitation (such as stirring) of the solvent. For example, a cube of zinc dissolves in HCl at a given rate. If the solution is left alone it will reach equilibrium when the rate at which particles of Zn leaving the cube equals the rate at which particles crystallized from the solution rejoin the cube.

Evidence of a chemical reaction

A gas may form or disappear, as when the calcium in an eggshell dissolves in vinegar's acetic acid (CH_3COOH). The gas appears as bubbles and will dissipate from an open container. A solid may form or disappear. When a lump of coal burns, the lump changes its form to ash, essentially disappearing. A liquid forms or disappears, as when flammable liquid burns, producing gases. A color change occurs, as when iron reacts with oxygen, producing rust. Energy is released as heat and/or light, as in the sudden

- 46 -

combustion of gunpowder. The temperature of a solution may drop when energy is absorbed in the form of heat from the surroundings. When vinegar reacts with $NaHCO_3$ (baking soda), the temperature of the solution drops because the reaction absorbs and metabolizes heat from the outside.

Transition state, intermediate, concerted reaction, and multi-step reactions

The transition state is the point of highest energy during a chemical reaction. Reactions exhibit differing energies—or enthalpies—as a reaction progresses; these differences are plotted as a curve in "reaction coordinate diagrams" and are one way of tracing the reaction rate. The transition state is the highest point on the plotted curve. An intermediate is a state of matter produced during a reaction that is neither reactant nor product, but something intermediary. They are typically highly unstable and exist for only a short time before becoming product. Concerted reactions are reactions in which bonds break and form simultaneously with no time interval or intermediates. Multi-step reactions require several steps to complete and often involve intermediates and enzymes, and may also depend on the polarity of the solution.

Reaction kinetics

"Reaction kinetics" is the study of the speed at which reactions occur and the sequence of bond formation and bond cleavage occurring in reactions. This concept is important because understanding the speed and sequence of reactions for a few samples of a given class of chemicals enables predictions about the reaction mechanisms of the entire class and compounds in which that class is found. "Kinetic" refers to motion and the energy inherent in moving bodies. Reactions occur when particles move about within a substance and react with one another, often using the kinetic energy as activation energy. The higher the speed of particles in motion, the higher the kinetic energy; this tendency explains why reactions often occur more quickly at higher temperatures.

Rate laws, first order reactions, second order reactions, and zero order reactions
Rate laws describe the relationship between the concentration of reactants and reaction rate. The relative speed of a reaction may increase with changes in reactant amounts; it may also decrease or show no impact. Rate laws track the effects of changes in reactant concentration on reaction rates. First order reactions are those reactions in which only a single reactant has an impact on reaction rate. The rate increases or decreases in direct proportion to the concentration of the reactant: doubling the concentration of reactant doubles the rate. Second order reactions are those in which both reactants impact the rate of reaction, and the relationship is not proportional, but exponential: doubling a reactant concentration raises the rate by four. Zero order reactions are those in which

changes in reactant concentration have no effect on reaction rate.

Reaction rates

Many factors influence the rate of chemical reactions, but the three most common factors are temperature, subdivision, and concentration:

- The higher the temperature, the faster the rate of reaction because reactant particles are moving more quickly and collide with other particles more often. Furthermore, particles are moving with greater energy at higher temperatures, increasing the chances that collisions result in reactions.
- Subdivision of reactants increases the rate of reaction because greater surface area means more particles are available to react. A solid block of baking soda will react with vinegar more slowly than powdered baking soda because less surface area is available, meaning fewer collisions of particles.
- Concentration of reactants influences the rate of reaction because greater concentration means more particles are present to collide and react with other particles.

Reaction rates can only be determined with certainty through experiments. Estimates can be made based on known properties of a compound, laws of equilibrium, and reaction conditions; but precise data only come from experiments. Some data considered in reaction kinetics are the amounts of reactant(s) and product(s), specifically the rate at which a reactant is being consumed (or changed via the reaction) and the rate at which product emerges. These amounts and the time period can then be plotted on graphs to provide a curve measuring the speed of the reaction. Measuring the concentration of a substance over time is another way to track a reaction's rate. For instance, the changes in volume of a product measured at ten minute intervals give an accurate average speed of reaction, assuming initial quantities are known.

Factors influencing rate
Chemical reactions can vary in how quickly they occur. These rates depend on many factors, including the following:

- The number of collisions of particles. Chemical reactions occur when electrons are transferred from one particle to another. Therefore, the greater the number of collisions between particles, the greater the transfer, or reactivity. Several factors determine the number of collisions including temperature (particles move faster and collide more at higher temperatures), concentration (more particles = more collisions), and the presence of other substances which facilitate collisions.
- The orientation of particles at the time of collision. Not all sites on a particle are reactive; if a collision

occurs at a non-reactive site, the reaction is impeded.

- The energy with which the collisions occur. Just as damage is greater in a car crash at higher speeds, greater energy is present when particles collide at higher velocities, increasing the reactivity.

Catalysis

Catalysis occurs when a catalyst is added to a reaction to increase its rate and efficiency. Catalysts change the rate of a reaction without being changed *by* the reaction and are important elements of chemical and biological processes. They function by decreasing the activation energy required for a reaction to occur. Homogeneous catalysis occurs when the catalyst is in the same state of matter as the reactant(s) and product(s). Heterogeneous catalysis occurs when the catalyst is in a different state. For example, hydrogen peroxide (H_2O_2) breaks down naturally to produce water and oxygen; this is normally a very slow reaction. Liquid hydrogen bromide can be added to the H_2O_2 to speed up the reaction considerably; because all compounds in question are liquid, this is an example of homogeneous catalysis. Solid manganese dioxide crystals (MnO_2) can also be added to the H_2O_2 as a catalyst to demonstrate heterogeneous catalysis.

Reaction enthalpy

Enthalpy is the expression of the chemical energy in elements and/or compounds, expressed in equations by H. Systems with high energy being said to have high enthalpy. This is measured by comparing the energy of a system to another whose enthalpy is known to be zero. The difference between the two gives the enthalpy of the system in which H is unknown, much as altitude is determined by using sea level as the constant 0 value. Because enthalpy (or the difference in enthalpy between products and reactants) is measured in final and initial states, the value will be the same regardless of reaction pathway. Enthalpy and its related measurements assume constant pressure. This is important to remember because all matter expends energy to "push back" against the atmosphere; enthalpy does not include this energy.

Le Châtelier's Principle

Le Châtelier's Principle states that a change in a system at equilibrium changes the concentrations of reactants or products and a new equilibrium results. For example, if more reactant is added to a system at equilibrium, a proportional change will be made to the product side of the reaction, resulting in a new equilibrium; the change in reactant is offset by the change in product to minimize the disturbance to the system. Similarly, if a product is removed from a chemical system in equilibrium, reactants create more product until equilibrium is restored. The volume of products and reactants has changed, but the constants and proportions will return to balance. The principle is useful to predict how changes to a system will influence products and reactants.

Chemical equilibrium

While reaction equilibrium is the law which states that the number of atoms present in reactants must equal the number of atoms present in the product(s), chemical equilibrium has to do with the rates of reactions. Many chemical reactions "recycle" their products into reactants, which then become products again. When the rate of production equals the rate at which products are broken into reactants, chemical equilibrium is reached. The state is represented by a double, bi-directional arrow: Ý. When both arrows are of equal length, the amount of product(s) and reactant(s), as well as the rate, are balanced. Greater quantities on either side of the equation may also be maintained by a system in equilibrium. If the system favors the product side, the top arrow is longer. A longer bottom arrow indicates greater volume of reactant(s) in a balanced system.

Equilibrium constants

The equilibrium constant is the data in equations which describes the interplay of reactants and products in a system at equilibrium. Once equilibrium has been reached, the concentration or reactants and products and the rate of reaction will remain constant if reaction conditions remain unchanged. The constant is represented as K in equations, and subscripts may be added to further describe the state and relation of compounds. K_c is used when concentrations of reactants and products are known, and K_p is used when the compounds involved are in the gaseous state. The subscript c represents concentration; when considering gases, pressure is a more useful measurement than concentration and is represented by the subscript p. Using the ideal gas law, K_c and K_p can be converted back and forth as necessary.

Oxidizing agent, reduction agent, and rate-determining step

An oxidizing agent is the reactant in oxidation reactions which gains electrons, causing oxidation of the other reactant(s). Peroxides, iodine and other halogens, and sulfoxides are common oxidizing agents. A reduction, or reducing agent, is the reactant oxidized in an oxidation reaction; it loses electrons to the oxidizing agent. In rusting iron, a common oxidation reaction, iron is the reducing agent, losing electrons to oxygen. In multi-step reactions, each of the steps has different reaction rates which are often very different. The rate-determining step is the slowest portion of such reactions. Because the reaction can only go as fast as its slowest step, that step determines overall reaction rate.

Electrophiles, nucleophiles, pericyclic reactions, and electrocyclic reactions

An electrophile is the acceptor of an electron pair in chemical reactions. A cation "seeks" additional electrons to balance its negative charge, so it is an electrophile. Nucleophiles are donors of electron pairs in reactions. Anions are nucleophilic because they "seek" a positively charged region near a nucleus to balance their negative charges. Pericyclic reactions are reactions whose defining characteristic is the reorganization of π and σ bonds through cyclic transition states. There are no intermediates in these reactions because electrons shift during the transition state to transform the reactant immediately to product. Or, the molecular orbitals of the reactant are transformed into the molecular orbitals of the product. Pericyclic reactions require activation energy, though not necessarily a great deal. Electrocyclic reactions are a class of exothermic pericyclic reactions in which a cyclic reactant is transformed into another cyclic product with one less double bond than the reactant.

Electrophilic and nucleophilic addition reactions

Addition reactions are those in which two reactants combine to yield a single product; they are characterized by the cleavage of double or triple bonds in the central molecule. Electrophilic addition reactions are those that depend upon the presence of an electrophile, often a proton. For example, in the addition reaction of HBr with an alkene, the alkene takes a proton from the HBr molecule (an acid) to form an intermediate C atom with a positive charge. That intermediate then combines with the Br- ion to form the final product—an alkane. Addition reactions are nucleophilic when a negative ion donates an electron pair at an electrophilic site, severing the double or triple bond to create a single product. In the reaction of HCl with an alkene, the C=C bond reacts with H to form H—C—H, a C^+ ion, and a Cl- ion, which donates an electron pair to C^+, neutralizing both ions.

Oxidation number

The oxidation number, or oxidation state, is a representation of the combination state of an element. Because elements produce different ions depending upon the compounds in which they occur and the types of bonds in which they are involved, the oxidation number identifies the ion in question. If the atom is isolated or in its uncombined state, the oxidation number is 0. The oxidation state of any given atom is given by the charge of the ion. For example, when fluorine occurs in ionic compounds, it is the fluoride ion, F-. When in covalent bonds, fluorine shares a single pair of electrons; the oxidation number -1 reflects this behavior. A single fluorine atom, uncombined with other elements has an oxidation number of 0. A calcium ion, Ca^{2+}, has an oxidation number of +2. The oxidation number enables accurate predictions for chemical reactions.

Electrochemistry

Electrochemistry describes the movement and generation of electrical charges or forces in chemical reactions. Electrical current can be used as activation energy as in electrolysis—the process of separating compounds into elements using electricity; for instance, water can be split into its constituent gases by passing an electrical current through it. Electricity can also be the desired product of reactions such as the acid reactions occurring inside batteries which gives them an electrical charge. Electricity can be envisioned as the movement of large numbers of electrons, all of which carry a negative electrostatic charge. The reactions in batteries break bonds and free electrons from their atoms so they can flow through conductors to the load, or destination of the electricity.

Voltaic cells

Voltaic cells, also known as galvanic cells, are important to electrochemistry because they were the first experiments to describe the flow of electricity produced by chemical reactions. They are the precursors of modern batteries. The cells involve two chemical mixtures and an oxidizing metal. In one mixture, a strip of solid zinc is placed in a zinc sulfate solution; and in the other, a strip of copper is placed in a solution of copper sulfate. An electrical current is generated by an oxidation reaction on the Zn side in which electrons are freed. A reduction reaction occurs on the Cu side, causing the solid Cu to gain electrons. A wire connects the two strips and allows electrons to move from the Zn side to the Cu side, generating an electrical current.

Redox chemistry

Redox chemistry is the branch of chemistry dedicated to the study of redox, or oxidation-reduction reactions. These reactions are also called displacement reactions because they are characterized by the replacement of one or more atoms in a compound with atom(s) of a different element. Redox reactions involve two halves—an oxidation occurs when one of the reactants loses electrons thus becoming positively charged. The partner in the reaction becomes reduced when it gains electrons and becomes negatively charged. Due to the transfer of electrons, all redox reactions involve changing the oxidation numbers of the reactants. The change in number is a more precise measurement of redox reactions, as the actual transfer of electrons may not occur; the charges are still generated because of the greater electronegativity of one of the reactants which draws its partner reactant's electrons closer to its nucleus.

Nonmetals

When nonmetal elements act as oxidizing agents, the nonmetal is reduced to a monatomic anion or a protonated form. The monatomic nonmetal anions and their protonated forms normally show the lowest oxidation number possible which allows them to transfer electrons back to other materials, or act as reducing agents. Nonmetals can be divided into two groups which are based on their redox properties. First, there are the very electronegative nonmetals. These nonmetals have an electronegativity of > 2.8 and are good oxidizing agents. Although O_2 is a strong oxidizing agent, it has oxidizing reactions that are normally slow kinetically. Many flammable materials exist in the presence of air until a reaction is started by a spark or flame. The second category of nonmetals is simply, electronegative nonmetals. These have electronegatives between 1.9 and 2.8. These are elements that have few uses in the laboratory as oxidizing agents.

Fermi energy

Fermi energy (EF) is the energy in a system of fermions that do not interact, has the smallest possible ground state energy (or its lowest energy state), and increases when only one particle is added to the system. It is equal to the chemical potential of the system in its ground state at absolute zero. It may also be seen as the maximum energy a single fermion can have in this ground state. Fermions obey Fermi-Dirac statistics, which is the statistical distribution of fermions over energy states in thermal equilibrium. The ground state of non-interacting fermion systems is built by beginning with an empty system and adding particles one after another and consecutively filling up the lowest-energy quantum states that are unoccupied. When the desired number of particles is reached, the Fermi energy is that of the highest occupied or lowest unoccupied state.

Conduction

Conduction in metals is due to electrons in conduction bands. Conduction in insulators is due to electrons in conduction bands and valence band holes. Holes are vacant states in valence bands that are removed when created. A

definition for the difference between insulators and semiconductors is electrons at ordinary temperatures can reach the conduction band. The probability that an electron reaches the conduction band is about exp(-Eg/2kT) where Eg is the band gap and kT has a usual meaning. In addition to having relatively small Eg, semiconductors have a covalent bond and insulators usually have a partial ionic bond.

Atomic spectra dynamics

Electrons in atoms have sets of allowed energy levels. They gain or lose energy by traveling between levels and absorbing emitting photons. Zero energy is achieved in an electron that is resting at infinity. Each atom has a different set of negative energies allowed. Atoms can drop from an allowed energy E1 to a lower E2 by the emission of a photon with energy.

$$hf = E1 - E2$$

Frequencies that correspond to the differences between allowed energies may be emitted. An atom can move to a higher allowed energy by absorbing an energized photon.

$$hf = E2 - E1$$

When atoms are close to each other, the energy level splits as electrons interact. In a solid, a continuous frequency range can be emitted or absorbed. Hot and dense materials emit continuous spectra that hold all frequencies. An example would be a light bulb filament emitting light at all frequencies.

Balmer and Rydberg equations

The Balmer formula is one of a set of six individual series that describes spectral line emissions of the hydrogen atom. Balmer saw a single number related to every hydrogen spectrum line in the visible light region. This number is 364.56 nm. The formula can be used for finding the wavelength of the absorption/emission lines and was originally written:
Where λ is the wavelength, h is a constant with a value of $3.6456 \times 10\text{-}7$ m or 364.56 nm; n is equal to 2; and m is an integer that is > n.

$$\lambda = B\left(\frac{m^2}{m^2 - n^2}\right) = B\left(\frac{m^2}{m^2 - 2^2}\right)$$

Rydberg made the formula for all transitions of hydrogen:

$$\frac{1}{\lambda} = R_{\text{H}}\left(\frac{1}{2^2} - \frac{1}{n^2}\right), n = 3, 4, 5, \ldots$$

Where λ is the wavelength of the absorbed/emitted light and RH is the Rydberg constant with the constant for an infinitely heavy nucleus is $3.6456 \times 10\text{-}7$ m or 364.56 nm.

H-alpha

H-alpha, also written, Hα, is an emission line that is created by hydrogen. Electrons exist in quantized energy levels that surround the atom's nucleus according to the Bohr model. The energy levels are described by the principal quantum number, n = 1, 2, 3 ... Electrons may only exist in these states and may only transition between states. The set of transitions from n ≥ 3 to n = 2 are the

Balmer series; n = 3 to n = 2 is known as Balmer-alpha or H-alpha; n = 2 is H-beta; n =5 to n = 2 is H-gamma and so on. The Lyman series is named n = 2 to n =1, known as Lyman-alpha; n =3 to n = 1 is Lyman-beta and so forth. H-alpha's wavelength of 656.3 nanometers is visible in the red portion of the electromagnetic spectrum.

Electron spin resonance

Electron spin resonance, ESR, is a spectroscopic technique used to detect species with unpaired electrons. Generally it means that it has to be a free radical of an organic molecule or a transition metal ion if it's an inorganic complex. Also known as electron paramagnetic resonance, EPR, the technique is rarely used in nuclear magnetic resonance (NMR) because most stable molecules have a closed-shell configuration without an appropriate unpaired spin. Weak magnetic fields and higher frequencies are used in comparison with NMR because of the difference in mass between the nuclei and electrons. ESR is used to identify and quantify radicals, or molecules with unpaired electrons. In chemistry it is used for identifying reaction pathways and is also used in medicine for biological spin probes.

Definitions of acids and bases

A definition of acids has historically been difficult to pin down. Several names and theories have been influential in expanding our understanding of acids, including the following: Arrhenius acids are named for Svante Arrhenius, who first described acids and bases as proton donors or hydroxide ion donors, respectively. His theory proposed that acids' unique properties come from the disassociation, or ionization, of H atoms when in aqueous solution. The Brønsted-Lowry theory overcomes some limitations of the Arrhenius definition by defining acids as proton donors and bases as proton acceptors.

The Lewis theory focuses on electron pairs as the defining components of acids and bases; it proposes that acids accept an electron pair while bases give them up. Each model has some limitations; some substances exhibit acidic or basic properties that are not explained by the most useful model for that substance. According to the Lewis theory of acids and bases, acids are substances whose atoms or molecules can accept an electron pair from another substance, forming a covalent bond. Lewis bases form covalent bonds by donating an electron pair. The properties of Lewis acids and bases therefore do not rely upon dissociation of ions, so do not have to include O or H like other acids. Any substance with an incomplete outer energy level (i.e., an incomplete octet) will tend to form covalent bonds by accepting electrons, and can thus be considered a Lewis acid. In this reaction, water acts as a Lewis acid by accepting an electron pair, while N is the Lewis base: $CN^- + H_2O$ Ý $HCN + OH-$

Physical properties of acids

Acids are a unique class of compounds characterized by consistent properties. The most significant property of an acid is not readily observable and is what gives acids their unique behaviors: the ionization of H atoms, or their tendency to dissociate from their parent molecules and take on an electrical charge. Carboxylic acids are also characterized by ionization, but of the O atoms. Some other properties of acids are easy to observe without any experimental apparatus. These properties include the following:

- A sour taste
- Change the color of litmus paper to red
- Produce gaseous H_2 in reaction with some metals
- Produce salt precipitates in reaction with bases

Other properties, while no more complex, are less easily observed. For instance, most inorganic acids are easily soluble in water and have high boiling points.

Common acids

Some common acids are often used in basic experiments because they are readily available and relatively safe and inexpensive. These useful acids include the following:

- Acetic acid. Formally known as ethanoic acid or methanecarboxylic acid; it is the acid responsible for the characteristic taste and smell of vinegar, household vinegar is simply acetic acid in aqueous solution. Its structural formula is CH_3COOH; its empirical formula is $HC_2H_3O_2$.

- Hydrochloric acid, HCl, is hydrogen chloride gas in aqueous solution. It is the main ingredient in gastric acid and has many industrial uses. It is highly corrosive, though not volatile by itself, so should be handled with appropriate lab safety precautions. It is nearly odorless.
- Nitric acid, HNO_3, is also a corrosive, strong acid with a sharp odor. It is used in the industrial production of fertilizers and explosives.

Acid/base strength

The characteristic properties of acids and bases derive from the tendency of atoms to ionize by donating or accepting charged particles. The strength of an acid or base is a reflection of the degree to which its atoms ionize in solution. For example, if all of the atoms in an acid ionize, the acid is said to be strong. When only a few of the atoms ionize, the acid is weak. Acetic acid ($HC_2H_3O_2$) is a weak acid because only its O2 atoms ionize in solution. Another way to think of the strength of an acid or base is to consider its reactivity. Highly reactive acids and bases are strong because they tend to form and break bonds quickly and most of their atoms ionize in the process.

Relationship to molecular geometry
Recall that the strength of an acid measures the tendency of its H (or O for carboxylic acids) atoms to ionize. In order to form the H^+ cation, a bond must be broken and particles transferred. Therefore, the easier it is to break this bond, the more acidic the substance will be. Molecular structure, or geometry, affects the ease with which bonds are broken in important ways. For instance, the size of the nonmetallic atom to which the H is bonded impacts bond strength because electrons in atoms with larger radii are more loosely held in orbit around the nucleus, leaving them vulnerable to reactions. Furthermore, the larger the molecule in which the H occurs, the easier it is for H^+ to separate from the molecule.

Hydrogen Theory of Acids

Hydrogen plays a central role in the modern understanding of acids and their properties; the set of ideas involving H atoms in acids is sometimes referred to as the Hydrogen Theory of Acids. These ideas focus on the hydrogen atom and its ability to dissociate, or separate from the rest of a molecule and become a H^+ cation. Not all H atoms in a substance can dissociate, and those that do can do so to different degrees—accounting for the relative "strength" or "weakness" of acids. An acid is said to be strong when all or most of its available hydrogen atoms dissociate and become H^+. Acids such as H_2SO_4 (sulfuric acid) and H_3PO_4 (phosphoric acid) containing more than one dissociable H atom are called polyprotic.

Acid/base properties of water

Depending upon the reaction in question, water can act as either an acid or a base, making it an amphoteric substance. Pure water in a closed system exists at an equilibrium within itself in which small portions of it self-ionize and then return to the neutral state. This self ionization equilibrium is the foundational reaction to all solution chemistry and is expressed: H_2O (l) Ý H + (aq) + OH^-(aq). The reactions below demonstrate this amphoterism. Water donates a proton in the first, making it an acid, and accepts a proton in the second, making it a base. NH_3(aq) + H_2O(l) Ý NH_4^+(aq) + OH^-(aq) HCl(g) + H_2O(l)→H_3O^+(aq) + Cl^-(aq)

Litmus and phenolphthalein

Litmus and phenolphthalein are both acid-base indicators. Litmus is a compound derived from certain types of lichens; it is often infused onto small strips of paper—litmus paper—for use in laboratory experiments. Litmus turns blue in contact with bases and red in contact with acids. It can also display a wide range of other colors indicative of various compounds and pH levels. Phenolphthalein ($C_{20}H_{14}O_4$) is an organic compound which also changes colors based on pH. In contrast to litmus, however, phenolphthalein is colorless in acid solutions and turns pink in basic solutions, with the color change occurring at around pH 8.3. It is also used industrially to make dyes and as a laxative, though toxic in large amounts. Indicators work through simple chemical changes and change colors because the changing molecular geometry in the reaction means the molecules reflect different wavelengths of light.

Neutralization

Neutralization is a chemical reaction that is also known as water-forming reaction. It is when an acid and a base reacts and produces a salt and water. It is a combination of hydrogen ions H+ and hydroxide ions OH- or oxide ions O2- to form water molecules (H2O). Salts are also formed during this process. Neutralization produces heat, or exothermic. The following normally occurs:

- Acid + Base --> Salt + Water : $\Delta H = -C < 0$

To use an example, take the reaction between sodium hydroxide and hydrochloric acid:

- hydrochloric acid + sodium hydroxide -> sodium chloride + water
- HCl(aq) + NaOH(aq) --> NaCl(aq) + H2O(l)

HCl and NaOH become ions in solution, so the ionic equation is:

- H+ + Cl− + Na+ + OH− --> Na+ + Cl− + H2O(l)

Since sodium and chloride ions are not involved in the reaction, the equation is:

- H+ + OH− --> H2O(l) : $\Delta Hr = -55.90$ kJ/mol

Krebs cycle

Also known as the citric acid cycle, the Krebs cycle is an important metabolic pathway in the series of pathways by which large molecules are broken down into energy for use by living organisms. It was named for its discoverer, Hans Adolf Krebs, who described the pathway in 1937. The cycle is the pathway in the metabolism of sugars. After a person eats a meal, for example, the food particles are converted to glucose and/or glycerol; they then undergo another pathway which further reduces the glucose/glycerol molecules to pyruvate, and then yet further to acetyl coenzyme A. That substance then enters the Krebs cycle where a complex series of reactions produce ATP (adenosine triphosphate), NAD (nicotinamide adenine dinucleotide), and NADP (nicotinamide adenine dinucleotide phosphate). A number of other pathways feed into the cycle at various points, providing necessary inputs and outputs for it and other pathways.

The citric acid (or Krebs) cycle takes place within the mitochondria of cells. It follows glycolysis and oxidative decarboxylation in the string of metabolic pathways through which sugars are converted to forms of energy usable by cells. It involves two rotations, or turns, through the cycle and begins when a molecule of acetyl coenzyme A (acetyl-CoA) forms citrate (a carboxylic acid also called citric acid) by reacting with a four-carbon carboxylate. A series of reactions converts the citrate back to a four-carbon carboxylate,

releasing CO_2 in the process and producing 1 ATP, 3 NADH, and 3 FADH. Because the input of pyruvic acid involves two molecules, the cycle "turns" again doubling the products to 2 ATP, 6 NADH, and 6 FADH. Water and 4 CO_2 are expelled as by-products.

Henderson-Hasselbalch equation

The Henderson-Hasselbalch equation describes the impact of pH on conjugate acid-base mixtures in equilibrium. More specifically, it derives the pH of a buffer without first having to calculate equilibrium. It is meant to simplify the calculation of pH and buffer strength by using small, positive numbers for constants instead of very small exponents (such as 10^{-14}) by taking the logarithm of the relative values of dissociated ions and their parent molecules. These numbers are represented in the equation by pKa and pKb. In each use of pK_a below, assume that pKb could be substituted. The full equation is as follows:

$$pH = pK_a + log\frac{[A^-]}{[HA]}$$

where A- is the anion of any hydrogen based acid. If A- and HA are equal, the pH and pK_a will be equal because the log of 1 is 0.

Bases

Basic chemicals are usually in aqueous solution and have the following traits: a bitter taste; a soapy or slippery texture to the touch; the capacity to restore the blue color of litmus paper which had

- 58 -

previously been turned red by an acid; the ability to produce salts in reaction with acids. "Alkali" is often used to describe bases. While acids yield hydrogen ions (H^+) when dissolved in solution, bases yield hydroxide ions (OH^-); the same models used to describe acids can be inverted and used to describe bases— Arrhenius, Brønsted-Lowry, and Lewis. Some nonmetal oxides (such as Na_2O) are classified as bases even though they do not contain hydroxides in their molecular form. However, these substances easily produce hydroxide ions when reacted with water, which is why they are classified as bases.

Neutralization reactions

Neutralization reactions are associated with acids and bases and are named as such due to the fact that the reaction cancels out, or neutralizes, the acidic and basic properties of the reactants. The foundation of neutralization reactions is the dissociation of water: $H_2O \acute{Y} H^+ + OH^-$; this ionization of water is the principal reaction of all aqueous acid-base reactions. According to the Arrhenius model, it is the only acid-base reaction (other theories are not so limiting). Neutralization reactions are exothermic and yield water and salts as in this example:

$$Na^+OH^- + HCl^- \rightarrow Na^+Cl^- + H_2O.$$
The salts produced in neutralization reactions are simply the ionic compounds of the anion and cation that were already present in the acid and the base. Because the reactions occur in solution, the salts are not solids, though some will

precipitate out of solution. The solid salts may be recovered by evaporating the water.

Buffering

Buffers are compounds, in solutions, which help to maintain the pH of that solution at an almost precise level despite other acids or bases that may be added. Solutions containing buffers are also sometimes called buffers, or are said to be "buffered." For example, if a solution containing a buffer has a pH of 5 (a fairly weak acid), the pH will not change appreciably if more acid—thus more dissociable H ions—are added to the mix. Buffers are usually made of a weak acid and the salt of that acid; the negative ions of the salts act as "ion traps" for the H+ which dissociate from the weak acid - they can't freely dissociate and change the pH of the solution. Buffer capacity is the upper limit of how much "protection" the buffer can provide; too much acid or base added to a solution will overwhelm the buffer.

Metabolism and homeostasis

Metabolism and homeostasis, present in all living things, are two essential functions for the maintenance of life.

Metabolism refers to the cell's ability to extract energy from its environment and use that energy for cell function, growth, and maintenance. The cell also uses this energy to reproduce itself as directed by DNA. Metabolism is a conversion of energy from external sources to fuel cell life. Photosynthesis is a prime example of cell metabolism. Light energy is converted to a specialized molecule, adenosine triphosphate (ATP), that the cell uses as a basic building block.

Homeostasis is the ability of a living cell to maintain an internal environment favorable to life. Internal systems ensure that a life form adjusts to changing conditions and survives. Examples are self-regulating thermostats in the body, which keep temperatures in a healthy range. Both simple and complex organisms have these internal controls that maintain homeostasis. Without this capacity, living beings could not survive changing conditions.

Organic synthesis and retrosynthesis

Organic synthesis is the chemical process by which organic and biomolecules are constructed. It is a large and growing branch of organic chemistry. Synthesis may be linear, in which complex molecules are the product of several intermediate steps in multi-step reactions; they may also be convergent, in which necessary parts of the molecule are created in separate reactions then brought together to from the desired product. Retrosynthesis refers to a methodology for the study of organic synthesis in which analysis begins with the products and works backwards, using known laws and steps to arrive at reactants. The Wöhler synthesis is an early example of attempts to understand organic synthesis. Organic synthesis occurs naturally in biological processes

and artificially in laboratories and industry, such as in the production of plastics and synthetic fibers.

Functional groups

"Functional groups" relate to organic chemistry; they are atoms or groups of atoms (two to four) within molecules which give the molecules their distinctive chemical reactions. Regardless of the other atoms surrounding the functional groups in a molecule, they will always react in the same or similar ways. Functional groups are the basis of nomenclature for organic compounds and are an important class of organic chemicals. Because their reactions are consistent and predictable, they are often the "pivot points" for discussions in organic chemistry. The presence of a functional group in a molecule defines that molecule as belonging to a specific chemical class. For example, organic molecules containing a hydroxyl group are classified as Alcohols. Some common functional groups are: Hydroxyl, Methyl, Alkyne, Amide, primary Amine, secondary Amine, tertiary Amine, Azo, Nitrite, Nitro, Nitroso, Pyridyl, Carboxyl, Aldehyde, and Ketone.

Chemical makeup
The following is a list of the chemical makeup of common functional groups:
- Hydroxyl: Characteristic of alcohols, the hydroxyl group is composed of an ion of OH single bonded to a hydrocarbon.
- Carbonyl: a C double bonded to an O forms a carbonyl, visually

represented: C=O, where the double line illustrates the double bond. Carbonyls with other atoms or simple molecules make up an important functional group including aldehydes, ketones, and esters.

- Carboxyl: A carbonyl that has reacted with an oxidizing agent and acquires an extra O is a carboxyl. In compounds they form an important class of organic acids called carboxylic acids.
- Amine: A base ammonia molecule (NH_3) in which one of the hydrogens has been replaced by an alkyl, forming $R—NH_2$, where R represents the alkyl.
- Esters: The product of a carboxyl's reaction with alcohol. The OH of alcohol and the H of the carboxyl condense to form water, leaving an ester: R—COO—R, where R represents any hydrocarbon to which the ester is bonded.

Classification of organic reactions

There are enormous numbers of known compounds and reactions important to organic chemistry. Classifying them is a necessary step in understanding and organizing them into usable information. The following categories are useful in such classification, although it is important to remember that each category contains various subcategories that further define the specific reactions:

- Structural change. These reactions include those in which reactants undergo structural changes. Four subclasses are in this category:

addition, elimination, substitution, and rearrangement.
- Reaction type, including acid-base, oxidation, and reduction reactions.
- Functional group. Many functional groups exist in organic chemistry, each with characteristic reactions. Just as organic nomenclature is based on which functional groups are present, reactions are also often determined by the functional group. Dehydration reactions, for instance, are typical of alcohols; while combustion reactions are typical of alkanes.

Wöhler synthesis

The Wöhler synthesis is an important reaction in the study of organic chemistry. Friedrich Wöhler synthesized urea, an organic compound, from inorganic elements (ammonium cyanate) in 1828, providing a key to the modern study of organic chemistry. Prior to Wöhler, chemists believed that organic compounds could not be synthesized and were animated by something called the "living force."

Alcohols

Composition and nomenclature

Alcohols are characterized by the functional group hydroxyl—OH—bonded to the parent hydrocarbon molecule. Alcohol is highly reactive because of the covalent bonds at both the C—O and O—H sites, which leave more "unattached" electrons free to engage in chemical reactions. This high reactivity accounts for the many uses of many types of alcohols, and its dangerous attributes. Alcohols are named by first identifying the parent hydrocarbon, usually an alkyl, and indicating the hydroxyl function by adding the –ol suffix, as in ethanol and propanol. Organic compounds may contain more than one hydroxyl group, these are called polyhydroxy alcohols. The reactions most often associated with alcohols have to do with the bonds of the –OH group. In some classes of alcohol reactions, the bond between the O and H is broken, while in others the bond between the O and C is broken, producing alkyl halides.

Physical and Analytical Chemistry

Heat and temperature

Temperature is the measure of the average energy of molecular motion within a substance. Heat is the total energy of molecular motion. Heat energy is dependent upon the speed of particles, the size or mass of the particles and what kind of particles are in an object. Temperature is not dependent upon types of objects or their size. Heat increases or decreases the temperature. If heat is added the temperature is higher. If heat is removed, then the temperature drops. Those higher temperatures signify molecular movement as well as vibration and rotation with more energy. Heat is energy while temperature is not energy but is instead a measure of it.

Thermocouple

A *thermocouple* is a type of temperature sensor that may also be used to convert thermal energy into electrical energy. This device can measure wide ranges of temperature, but is prone to inaccuracy. The thermocouple works on the principle that when any conductor (such as a metal) is subject to a thermal gradient, it will generate a small amount of voltage. This is called the Peltier-Seebeck effect, and is a direct conversion of heat differentials to electric voltage, or the reverse. In order for a thermocouple to produce an output voltage, there must be a temperature difference between the junction of two metal wires.

Temperature

Temperature is a thermodynamic property of a substance. The temperature of a substance depends upon its energy content. The two most commonly employed temperature scales are Fahrenheit and Celsius. In the Fahrenheit scale, water freezes at 32°; in the Celsius scale, it freezes at 0°. There are also two absolute scales of temperature, which are used to define the temperature independent of the properties of the substance. The absolute scale in the U.S. system is the Rankine scale, and the absolute scale in the SI system is the Kelvin scale.

Specific heat of metal

Measurement of the specific heat of metals such as copper can be done by placing the metal into a calorimeter that contains water at a different temperature than the metal. If the copper is at first a higher temperature than the water, the heat will transfer from the copper to the water. While the metal is cooling, the water will warm. As both reach similar temperatures no more heat transfers. The calorimeter minimizes heat loss to surroundings. Heat that is gained by the water will be equal to the heat lost by the copper. The mass and initial temperature of both the water in the calorimeter and the copper must be measured first. The copper is put into boiling water long enough to reach the temperature of the water and then is put quickly into the calorimeter. Once water and copper reach equal temperatures, the final temperature reading is taken.

Joule

The joule, expressed as "J," is the SI unit of energy or work. It was named after physicist James Joule. It is a derived unit that reflects the work done or energy required to exert a force of one newton for a distance of one meter. The same quantity could also be referred to as a newton meter with a symbol N-m. The newton meter is normally utilized to measure torque instead of energy. One joule is the absolute minimum amount of energy that is required on the Earth's surface to lift a one-kilogram object 10cm. It is the equivalent of about 2.390×10^{-4} calorie or 9.48×10^{-4} BTU.

Absolute zero

Absolute zero is the lowest possible temperature that is obtained when a system is at its minimum possible energy. The Kelvin scale has its zero point at absolute zero which is -273.15 on the Celsius scale and -459.67 Fahrenheit. A true minimum has been confirmed by a number of experiments. Since temperature is molecular energy then it would follow that there must be a certain point at which no additional energy could be taken from a system. It is possible to approach absolute zero, yet the Third Law of Thermodynamics says that absolute zero cannot be reached in a system.

Cosmic background radiation, which are relic photos left over from the very early and hot phase of the Big Bang, has a temperature of about 2.7 degrees above absolute zero.

Calorimeter

A calorimeter is an object that is used for measuring the heat of chemical reactions or physical changes. A calorimeter might be composed of just a thermometer attached to an insulated container. In order to find the enthalpy change per mole of a substance X in a reaction between the liquids X and Y, they are added to the calorimeter and the first and last temperatures are recorded. A value for the energy given off during a reaction, if that reaction was exothermic, can be found by multiplying the temperature change by the mass and specific heat capabilities of the liquid. The enthalpy change of reaction can be found by dividing the energy change by the number of moles X present.

Mercury-in-glass thermometer

The mercury-in-glass thermometer uses mercury in a glass tube. It contains marks on the tube that are calibrated and allow the temperature to be seen by the length of the mercury inside the tube. That length will vary according to temperature. A bulb is usually at the base of the thermometer in order to increase the sensitivity of the instrument. The bulb contains most of the mercury. The expansion and contraction of the volume of mercury is amplified in the bore of the tube, which is much more narrow than the bulb. The space that is above the mercury may be a vacuum or it might be filled with nitrogen. Mercury freezes at -38.83 degrees C or 37.89 degrees F. Therefore, it can only be used at temperatures higher than 37.89 degrees F. Since mercury does not expand when frozen, like water, it will not break the glass tube.

Internal energy, thermal energy, and heat

A distinction is made in physics between heat, internal energy and thermal energy. Internal energy is all of the energy that belongs to a stationary system. This includes thermal energy, nuclear energy and chemical energy. The motion or interaction between atoms comprising the system is internal energy. If an outside or external object is involved in the interaction then it is not included in the internal energy. Thermal energy is the portion of internal energy that is changed when the phase of a substance changes or the temperature changes. This is due to the kinetic energies, or motion energies that are associated with the atoms' random motions in a system. Heat is simply the measure of thermal energy transfer, representing the change in thermal energy.

Heat conduction

Conduction is one method of heat transfer and happens when there is molecular agitation without motion of the material. For instance, if one end of a metal rod has a higher temperature, then energy will transfer down that rod toward the colder portion because higher speed particles will connect with slower ones that will result in a net transfer of energy to the slower ones. In the heat transfer between two plane surfaces, such as in heat loss through the wall of a home, the conduction heat transfer rate variables are: Q = heat transferred in time = t; k = thermal conductivity of the barrier; A = area; T = temperature; d = barrier thickness.

The rate of the heat transfer is dependent upon temperature gradient and thermal conductivity of a specific material.

Heat convection

Convection is another heat transfer method. The heat is carried by the mass motion of a fluid such as water when the heated fluid is moved away from the heat source and carries energy along with it. Convection occurs above a hot surface because hot air expands, becomes less dense and also rises. Hot water is less dense than cold water and rises. This causes convection currents transporting energy. Convection can also cause circulating liquid as in a heated pot of water over a fire. Heated water will expand and become more buoyant. The more dense, cooler water near the surface descends and circulation patterns may form. Convection is believed to be a major factor in the transportation of energy from the center of the Sun to its surface.

Misunderstandings about heat energy

Students may believe that heat and temperature are the same thing. They may think that heat and cold are similar quantities but opposite. They may believe ice cannot be cooled below freezing. Their beliefs may also include the thought that the temperature of water cannot be higher than its boiling point. They may think that the temperature always rises when a mixture is heated. Or they could think that heat rises and energy may only go up. They may mistakenly think that bubbles in boiling water are air or that you can tell the temperature of an object by the way it feels. Students may also hold views that while matter contains particles it does not consist exclusively of particles. They may think particles are all the same size and about the size of cells or perhaps a bit smaller.

Relative humidity

Relative humidity is the percent of saturation humidity that is calculated generally in relation to saturated vapor density.
Relative Humidity = actual vapor density/saturation vapor density x 100 percent
Evaporation in a closed container will proceed until as many molecules return to the liquid as escape. At this point, the vapor is said to be saturated. The pressure of that vapor, which is usually expressed in mmHg, is the saturation vapor pressure. Molecular kinetic energy is greater at higher temperatures, so more molecules may escape to the surface. The saturated vapor pressure corresponds as higher as well. If the liquid is open then vapor pressure is viewed as a partial pressure along with the other constituents of the air. The boiling point is the temperature at which the vapor pressure equals the atmospheric pressure.

Kinetic molecular theory

The kinetic molecular theory is based on these postulates:
- Gases are composed of a large number of particles. They behave like hard, spherical objects that are constantly in a state of random motion.
- These particles move in a straight line until they have a collision with another particle or the walls of the container.
- These particles are much smaller than the distance that is between the particles. Most of the volume of the gas is empty space.
- There is no force of attraction between the particles and the walls of the container or between gas particles.
- Collisions between gas particle or with the walls of a container are elastic. A gas particle loses no energy when it collides with another particle or the walls of the container.
- The average kinetic energy of a gas particle collection depends on the gas' temperature and nothing else.

The assumptions of the kinetic molecular theory can be shown in an experiment with a glass plate surrounded by walls that are mounted on top of three vibrating motors. About a handful of ball bearings are placed on top of the glass. This represents the gas particles. When the motors are started, the glass plate vibrates. This makes the ball bearings move in a random, constant way. Each ball moves in a straight line until colliding with another ball or with the walls. The collisions are frequent but the average distance between the ball bearings is much larger than the ball's diameter. There is no force of attraction between the individual ball bearings and the wall. Any object in motion has a kinetic energy that is defined as half the product of its mass times its velocity squared:
$KE = 1/2\ mv2$

Amontons' Law

Amontons' law is another postulate of the kinetic molecular theory. It states that the average kinetic energy of a gas particle is dependent upon the temperature of the gas. Consequently, the average kinetic energy of the gas particles increase as the gas gets warmer. Because the mass in these particles is constant, their kinetic energy will only increase if there is an increase in the average velocity of the particles. The faster that the particles move when they hit the wall, the greater the force that will be exerted on the wall. Since the force of each collision gets larger as the temperature rises, the gas pressure must also increase

Gibbs' Phase Rule

The phase rule, postulated by J.W. Gibbs in the 1870s, is a description of the possible number of degrees of freedom in a closed system that is at equilibrium.

The rule is: $F = C - P + 2$

Description of Variables:

- F = The degrees of freedom. This is the number of intensive variables and those that are independent of the quantity of material present that need values specified to fully determine the state of the system. Variables might include pressure, concentration or temperature.
- P = Phase. The phase is a component of the system that cannot be mixed or blended with other parts such as a gas, liquid or solid. A phase may contain several chemical constituents. Those may or may not be shared with other phases.
- C = Chemical Constituents. These are the distinct compounds, or elements, that are part of the equation of the system. If some of the constituents stay in equilibrium with each other, regardless of the state of the system, then they should be considered a single constituent.

Graham's Laws of Diffusion

Some physical properties of gases are dependent upon their identity as a gas. Thomas Graham, in 1829, used an apparatus to study the diffusion of gases, or the rate at which two gases will mix. Using a similar apparatus can exemplify this diffusion. By taking an apparatus consisting of a glass tube that is sealed at one end with plaster and has holes large enough to allow gas to enter or leave the tube and filling it with Hydrogen gas, the water level rises slowly because the hydrogen gas molecules escape through the holes in the plaster faster than the molecules in the air can enter the tube. Graham was able to obtain information on the rate at which gases mix by studying the rate at which water levels rose. Graham's law states that the rates at which gases diffuse is inversely proportional to the square root of their densities.

Graham's Law of Effusion

Thomas Graham studied the rate of gas effusion, which is the rate at which gas will escape through a pinhole into a vacuum. The rate of gas effusion is inversely proportional to the square root of either the gas density or the molecular weight of the gas. To show this: A filter flask is evacuated with a vacuum pump. A syringe is filled with 25 mL of gas. The time required for the gas to escape through the syringe needle and into the evacuated filter flask is measured with a stop watch. The results can show that the time required for the 25-mL samples of different gases to escape is proportional to the square root of the molecular weight. Graham's observations about the rate at which gases mix, or diffuse, or effuse suggest that particles of gas which are relatively light such as H2 or He move faster than heavier gas particles such as CO2 or SO2.

Avogadro's law of gases

Avogadro's law relates the volume and number of molecules of a gas. It holds that equal volumes of different gases contain the same number of molecules. The volume of any given gas is proportional to the number of molecules present. This is a minor aspect of the law:

$$\frac{V}{n} = a$$

where V is the volume of the gas; n is the number of moles in the gas; and a is a constant. Most important is that the ideal gas constant has the same value for all gases. This means:

$$\frac{p_1 \cdot V_1}{T_1 \cdot n_1} = \frac{p_2 \cdot V_2}{T_2 \cdot n_2} = const$$

has the same value for all gases regardless of the gas molecule size.

Ideal gas

A gas can be considered ideal if its pressure is very low and its temperature is higher than its critical temperature. This allows the molecular radius to be considered insignificant compared to the distance between molecules. It can also be assumed that the molecules do not come into contact with each other. Typically, highly superheated vapors are considered ideal gases. Avogadro's law states that equal volumes of different gases at the same temperature and pressure contain equal numbers of molecules. This is represented for n moles of any gas as the

- 68 -

equation of state for ideal gases, or the ideal gas law:

$$PV = nRT$$

Where P = pressure, V = volume, n = number of moles, R = universal gas constant, T = temperature.

Kinetic gas theory

Kinetic gas theory maintains that gas pressure is the result of collisions between molecules and the walls of the container in which they exist. The total pressure depends upon the frequency of collision per unit area and the force with which the molecules strike the wall. The following assumptions are central to the theory:

- The gas molecules neither attract nor repel one another.
- The distance between the molecules is considered much greater than the size of the molecules. In other words, the molecules can be considered to be points possessing mass but with negligible volume.
- Gas molecules are in a state of constant, random motion. Collisions are perfectly elastic and although energy is transferred from one molecule to another because of the collision, the total energy of the system remains constant.
- The average kinetic energy of the molecules is proportional to the temperature in Kelvins. Two different gases will have the same kinetic energy provided they are at the same temperature.

Boyle's law of gases

Boyle's law relates the pressure and volume of a gas. It states that the volume of a gas and its pressure are inversely related:

$$PV = k$$

where V is volume; P is pressure; and k is constant. Given a fixed amount of gas at a constant temperature, the volume is inversely proportional to the gas pressure. The volume and pressure are usually related by a constant, k1, called the proportionality constant. This says that the product of the pressure and volume of a fixed amount of gas at constant temperature is constant.

Charles' law of gases

Charles' law relates the temperature and volume of a gas. It states that the volume of a gas and its temperature are directly proportional:

$$\frac{V}{T} = k$$

Where V = volume; T = temperature; and k is a constant. Given a fixed amount of gas at a constant pressure, the volume is directly proportional to the absolute temperature of the gas. The volume and temperature are often related by a constant, k2, called the proportionality constant:

Pressure-volume relationship with gas

Gas molecules that are inside a fixed volume, such as a balloon, are constantly moving around freely. During this molecular motion, they often collide with

- 69 -

each other and with the surface of any enclosure that might be there. The force of impact of a single collision is too minuscule to be sensed. But the large number of impacts of gas molecules will exert a sizable force onto the enclosure's surface. The larger the number of collisions per area of enclosure, the larger the pressure. The SI unit of pressure is Pa, or Pascal. In meteorology the use of millibars (mb) is accepted where 100 kPa = 1000 millibars. The direction of this gas pressure force is always perpendicular to the surface of the enclosure at all points.

Gay-Lussac's Law

Gay Lussac's discovered two laws. One states that between combining volumes of gases and the product, the ratio can be expressed in small whole numbers. Avogadro used this data to form his hypothesis. This paved the way for modern gas stoichiometry, or the quantitative relationship between products and reactants within a chemical reaction. Another Gay-Lussac Law states that the pressure of a fixed amount of gas at volumes that are fixed is directly proportional to its temperature in kelvins. It is expressed:

$$\frac{P}{T} = k$$

P is the gas pressure; T is the gas temperature in kelvins; k is a constant. The law is true because temperature is a way to measure average kinetic energy of a substance. As a gases' kinetic energy increases, a collision occurs between its particles and the container walls more rapidly, causing an increased pressure.

Hydrostatic pressure

The principle that at a given level the pressure is equivalent to the weight of the overlying column is true for gases and liquids. The pressure generated by an overlying fluid column is called hydrostatic pressure. The air column's upper boundary that causes a rise in atmospheric pressure is the vacuum of space. Being somewhat light, the mass of an air column with a 1 cm2 cross section is almost exactly 1 kg. If a heavier liquid substance is used in balancing this air column, a relatively small length would be required. Additionally, the density of liquids does not change with height as most liquids are incompressible, so an equivalent liquid column has a well-defined upper boundary below a vacuum.

Compressibility of gas

When an object moves through a gas, the compressibility of the gas becomes an important factor. Gas molecules move around an object as it passes through. If an object passes by at a low speed, usually below 200 mph, the density of the fluid remains constant. For higher speeds, some of the energy of the object will go into compression of the fluid, moving molecules closer together and causing a change in the gas density. This alters the amount of force that results on the object. The effect becomes of more importance as speed is increased. Near and beyond the speed of sound, 700 mph, shock waves are produced. They affect both the lift and drag of objects.

Dalton's Law of Partial Pressure

Dalton's Law of Partial Pressure states that the total pressure that is exerted by the mixture of different gases in an gas volume is equal to the sum of the partial pressures of each individual component in the overall gas mixture. The law also states that each individual component in any mixture of gas exerts its own individual partial pressure, in the exact ratio as its mole fraction -- or volume-based concentration -- in the particular mixture. The relationship gives a way to determine a volume-based concentration of any individual gas components in a mixture of several other gases that are in air.

Enthalpy of phase changes

Enthalpy (symbol H and also known as heat content) is the sum of the internal energy of matter and the product of its volume multiplied by the pressure. The enthalpy of phase changes include vaporization, fusion and sublimation. The difference in enthalpy per mole of molecules between a gaseous and liquid state of a substance is known as the enthalpy of vaporization, or Hvap. The difference in enthalpy per mole of molecules between the liquid and solid states of a substance is known as the enthalpy of fusion, or Hfus. The difference in enthalpy per mole of molecules between the gaseous and solid states of a substance is called the enthalpy of sublimation, or Hsub.

Spontaneous processes

A spontaneous process is a chemical reaction in which a system releases free energy, usually heat, and goes to a lower and more thermodynamically stable state of energy. For reactions at constant temperatures and pressures where:

$$\Delta G = \Delta H - T\Delta S$$

- A negative ΔG depends on the sign changes in enthalpy (ΔH), entropy (ΔS) and the magnitude of the Kelvin absolute temperature.
- Changes of ΔG will not experience a direct change by temperature because it is never less than zero.
- When ΔS is positive and ΔH is negative, a spontaneous process occurs.
- When ΔS is positive and ΔH is positive, a process is spontaneous at high temperatures, where exothermicity has a small part in the balance.
- When ΔS is negative and ΔH is negative, a process is spontaneous at low temperatures, where exothermicity is a major factor.
- When ΔS is negative and ΔH is positive, a process is not spontaneous at any temperature, but there is a reverse spontaneous process.

Entropy

Entropy is a thermodynamic measurement of the amount of energy in a physical system that cannot be used to do work in a closed system. It is a key physical variable used in the description of a thermodynamic system. The SI unit of entropy is joules per kelvin; this is the same unit used for heat capacity. Entropy depends upon the current state of a system rather than its past history. In a process where the system gives up an energy ΔE, and its entropy falls by ΔS, a quantity at least TR ΔS of that energy must be given up to the system's surroundings as unusable heat (TR is the temperature of the system's external surroundings, which need not be the same as the system's current temperature T); Otherwise the process will not go forward.

Equipartition theorem of energy

The theorem of equipartition of energy states that molecules in thermal equilibrium have the same average energy associated with each independent degree of freedom of their motion. In thermodynamics the equipartition theorem says that the mean internal energy that is associated with each degree of freedom of a monatomic ideal gas is the same. For a molecule of gas, each component of velocity will have an associated kinetic energy.

Energy distribution function

The distribution function f(E) is the probability that a particular particle is in energy state E. The distribution function generalizes ideas of probability to where energy can be treated as a variable that is continuous. There are three distinct and different distribution functions: Maxwell-Boltzmann deals with particles that are identical but are also distinguishable. An example is the distribution of molecular speed. Bose-Einstein functions are directed at those particles that are indistinguishable with integer spin. Thermal radiation is an example. The Fermi-Dirac is concerned with identical and indistinguishable particles with a half-integer spin. An example would be electrons in a metal.

Maxwell-Boltzmann Distribution

The Maxwell-Boltzmann distribution is a classical distribution function for the distribution of a quantity of energy between identical particles that are distinguishable.
Certain classical statistical physicists surmise that:

- No restriction exists on the number of particles occupying a given state.
- The distribution of particles, at thermal equilibrium, among available energy states takes the most probable distribution that is consistent with the total available energy as well as the total amount of particles.

It is unlikely one particular particle will get an energy that is well above the average. Energies that are lower than average are more in favor because of more ways to get them. If a particle gets an energy of 10 times the average, then it will reduce the number of possibilities for the distribution of the remaining energy. It is thus unlikely because the probability of occupying a given state is proportional to the different ways it can be obtained.

Science of thermodynamics

Thermodynamics as a science investigates and analyzes thermal paths that lead from an energy source, such as a form of fuel, to useful work. The development of equipment that operates over thermal paths that are close to theoretical ones is sometimes viewed as an art. Nonetheless, the two are distinct and studying them separately help to give a better application of theoretical relationships to the problems involved in practical design. One reason is that theories can become obsolete more slowly than equipment. Also, a deep knowledge of thermodynamics is needed to relate to the equipment of today, yesterday and tomorrow. Thermodynamic study begins with the sources of energy and then leads to one of the many thermal paths that end up as the desired product or mechanical work. While a number of steps are required for conversion, each step is purposeful in liberation, storage, transportation, transformation, transfer or the utilization of energy.

Intensive and extensive properties

The thermodynamic state of a substance is determined by its properties. Intensive properties are independent of the quantity of material making up the system. Examples of intensive properties are temperature, pressure and stress. Extensive properties are dependent upon the quantity of material involved. Examples of extensive properties are volume, density, mass, charge, and strain.

Thermodynamic process

The thermodynamic process is defined as the series of continuous states that are followed by a working substance it liberates, transforms, transfers or receives energy from. A major problem in thermodynamics is classifying the different types of processes and picking the ones providing the best theoretical applications. Under constant conditions, three measurable properties exist. One is an isothermal process that occurs without a change in temperature. Another is an moist process which takes place at a constant pressure. There is also an isometric process which is a process of constant volume. An example of isothermal is when energy is added to ice and melting occurs. Isopiestic is represented by expansion against atmospheric pressure. Isometric processes are those that correspond to heating a material that is inside a rigid and nonexpanding container.

Independent thermodynamic properties and intensive state

The number of independent thermodynamic properties required to establish the intensive state of any system can be determined using the phase rule:
$$F = 2 - P + N$$
where P = number of phases, N = number of chemical species. For a pure homogeneous substance, P = 1, N = 1

- 73 -

therefore the number of independent thermodynamic properties, or degrees of freedom, F, that must be defined to fix its state is 2.

Phase rule variables are intensive properties and are independent of the extent of the system and the individual phases. As such, the information given by the phase rule is independent of both the size of the system and the amounts of the phases present.

First Law of Thermodynamics

The first law of thermodynamics in its simplest form holds that energy cannot be either created or destroyed. If energy enters a system it must leave the system or be stored in the system in some manner. Stated another way, the total quantity of energy is constant and when energy disappears in one form it simultaneously appears in another form. The work done in an adiabatic process depends only on the end conditions and not the nature of the process. The first law can be written as follows:

$$E = Q - W$$

Where Q is heat; E is energy; and W is work.

Second Law of Thermodynamics

The second law of thermodynamics restricts the direction in which heat and energy can flow. It has been stated in many ways, a very common and simple one is:
No process is possible which consists solely in the transfer of heat from one temperature level to a higher one. Stated another way, it is impossible to convert heat absorbed by a system completely into work done by the system. This means that the net entropy of a process will always increase and will proceed in the direction which causes the entropy of the system and surroundings to increase.

Third Law of Thermodynamics

The Third Law of Thermodynamics states that as a system approaches absolute zero of temperature all processes cease and the entropy of the system approaches a minimum value, or zero for the case of a perfect crystalline substance. The law states that the entropy of the system at absolute zero temperature is a constant that is well defined. At zero temperature, a system exists in its ground state; entropy is determined by how the ground state degenerates or it would be impossible to reduce any system to absolute zero in a finite number of operations. This law gives a reference point that is absolute for determining entropy. The entropy that is determined to be relative to this point is the absolute entropy.

Zeroth Law of Thermodynamics

The "Zeroth" law states that if two systems are in thermal equilibrium at the same time with a third system, then they are in thermal equilibrium with each other. If A and C are in thermal equilibrium with B, then A is in thermal equilibrium with B. In practicality, this says that all three are the same temperature. This forms a basis to compare temperatures. Any system with a number of microscopic parts, such as a gas, that is isolated from all forms of energy exchange and left alone for quite awhile will move toward a state of thermal equilibrium. A system in thermal equilibrium is characterized by a set of quantities that are macroscopic and are dependent on the system in question and characterizes its state. Two systems are in equilibrium, if when put in thermal contact with each other, their variables do not change.

Bridgman's Thermodynamic equations

Bridgman's Thermodynamic equations produce a large number of thermodynamic identities that involve a number of thermodynamic quantities. The variables are:

- U = Internal energy
- F = Hemholtz free energy
- G = Gibbs free energy
- H = Enthalpy
- N = Particle number
- P = Pressure
- p = Density
- S = Entropy
- T = Temperatures
- Cv = Heat capacity, constant volume
- Cp = Heat capacity, constant pressure

Many thermodynamic equations are expressed in terms of partial derivatives. The partial derivative of enthalpy with respect to temperature while holding pressure constant may be written as:

$$C_P = \frac{(\partial H)_P}{(\partial T)_P}$$

Rewriting of the partial derivative allows the use of many thermodynamic equations such as:

$$(\partial H)_P = C_P$$

Chemical potential energy and electromagnetic potential energy

Everything has molecules. Energy is required to make these molecules and hold them together. The energy stored in molecules is called chemical potential energy. An example is the energy stored in gasoline. Bonds are broken and reformed during combustion and new products are made. The energy stored in gasoline is released when it is burned, which is combustion. Gasoline is changed into byproducts during combustion such as water and carbon dioxide, and energy is released. An airplane motor will use the energy that is released to turn a propeller. A battery has chemical potential energy as well as electrical potential energy. When a flashlight is turned on, the electrical potential energy stored in the battery is converted into other forms of energy such as light. With an electrical appliance that is plugged in, electrical potential energy is maintained in a power plant's generator, a windmill or a hydroelectric dam.

Adhesion

The molecular attraction that is exerted between bodies when in contact is called adhesion. Five types of adhesion exist.

Mechanical adhesion is when two materials become mechanically interlocked. An example is sewing. Chemical adhesion is when two materials form a compound at the joint. The strongest joints are where atoms from the two materials have an ionic bonding or covalent bonding of outer electrons. Dispersive adhesion, also known as adsorption, is when two materials are held together by what is known as "van der Waals forces." These forces are attractions between two molecules that have ends that are both positively and negatively charged. Electrostatic adhesion occurs when conducting materials pass electrons to each other forming a difference in electrical charge at the joint. The final type of adhesion his when materials merge at the joint by diffusion.

Chemical bonds

Chemical energy and bond energy
Chemical energy is the latent, or potential energy contained in atoms and molecules resulting from the forces within them. While the precise chemical energy of a given particle or substance cannot be determined, the difference in energy between one chemical state and another can be readily calculated and expressed as enthalpy. When chemical energy is lower, the particle is said to be in an unexcited, or stable state, and is less likely to create or sever bonds. Bond energy is the potential energy stored in chemical bonds. Chemical reactions involve the exchange of energy as bonds are created and/or broken. This exchange is measured in calories (an English system

measurement) and joules (a metric unit of measurement). The heat and light produced by combustion of natural gas is an example of the release of chemical and bond energy.

Types and properties
Chemical bonds are the forces which hold atoms together in molecules and compounds. Three common types are:

- Ionic bonds: atoms are attracted to one another by electrostatic forces due to the opposite charges of their ions. Inorganic binary compounds composed of a metal and a non-metal are typically formed with ionic bonds because the metal loses an electron, gaining a positive charge, while the non-metal gains the electron, resulting in a negative charge.
- Covalent bond: atoms share, or swap, one or more pairs of electrons in their outer shells, producing a bond of roughly the same strength as ionic bonds.
- Metallic bond: a relatively weak bond formed by electrostatic attraction between a metal atom's core and its outer-level electrons. The outer energy levels of individual atoms essentially overlap, allowing valence electrons to easily transfer from one atom to another. These weak bonds account for the low melting point and malleability of most metals.

Chemical reactivity

Chemical reactivity refers to the tendency of a given element or compound to be involved in chemical reactions. As chemical reactions are essentially the transfer of electrons to form or break chemical bonds, producing new elements or compounds, the bonds present between molecules are important factors in determining reactivity. Weak bonds and unstable (unbalanced) molecules lend themselves more readily to chemical reactions, while strong bonds and stable molecules are less likely to react without significant external activation energy. For example, hydrocarbons vary in the number of bonds between atoms of H and O; molecules in which the H and O are connected with double or triple bonds are less likely to react at that site. Other components of the molecule may be very reactive, but the double and triple bonds are stable and require a great deal of energy to break.

Molecular geometry

Molecules are groups of atoms bound by overlapping energy levels which have a specific orientation in three-dimensional space. The resulting molecule has a three dimensional shape which we can imagine as straight lines between the nuclei of bonded atoms. Molecular geometry, or molecular shape, refers to the characteristic shapes of molecules. These shapes are determined by the number and type of atoms present and the type(s) of bonds connecting them. A water molecule, for example, is bent, or v-shaped, with the two H atoms bonded at angles to a central O atom. The positions and angles of a molecule's bonds are predictable because electron pairs repel one another and arrange themselves around the central atom to be as far away from each other as possible. Common molecular shapes include tetrahedral, linear, angular, and pyramidal.

States of matter

All matter is known to have various forms, or states, of existence—solid, liquid, and gas. These states are in large part determined by the atomic properties of the elements and compounds and their bonding propensities. Atoms and molecules in a solid exist in a low energy state in which their movement is greatly decreased. They align themselves into consistent organizations in which intramolecular bonds play an important role. Because of the decreased kinetic energy, bonds in solids are relatively stable and require external energy to change them. Particles in a gaseous state move rapidly and randomly, increasing the chances that bonds will be made or broken. The kinetic energy of liquid particles is smaller than in gasses and greater than in solids. Because their motion is slower and less random, they condense into the characteristic form of liquids but do not align themselves so neatly as to form solids.

Ionization energy

The ionization energy of an atom or molecule, also called ionization potential, is the energy required to strip the atom or molecule of one electron. The nth ionization energy is the energy required to strip it of an nth electron, after the first, n - 1, is already removed. It is a measure in physical chemistry of the reluctance of an atom or molecule to give up an electron or the strength by which the electron is anchored. Generally, ionization energies decrease down a group of the periodic table and increase from left to right across a period. Ionization energy has a strong negative correlation with the atomic radius. Atomic ionization energy can be predicted by an analysis that uses the Bohr model and electrostatic potential, or the potential energy per unit of charge that is associated with a static electric field.

Chemical bonds

Molecular orbitals

Molecular orbitals describes the probable location of electrons in a molecule. Atomic orbitals are the probable locations of electrons within atoms. They are envisioned and represented as spherical, oval, and teardrop-shaped regions of space which together form the molecule's geometry. They are formed by arranging constituent atomic orbitals in a linear plane with varying degrees of overlap to demonstrate sharing of electrons between atoms. The overlap of two atomic 1s orbitals, represented as spheres, produces an oval-shaped molecular orbital which is symmetrical around the two nuclei. The new orbital is called a sigma (denoted by the Greek letter σ) molecular orbital. When two 2p orbitals overlap, the resulting molecular orbital is not symmetrical, and is called a pi (π) molecular orbital. The larger the

area of overlap, the stronger the resulting chemical bond. This theory partially explains the strength of CH bonds in hydrocarbons; they are σ molecular bonds.

Hybridization

Orbital hybridization is the mixture, or shifting, of ground state orbitals within an atom which permits the formation of the necessary number of bonds to meet the octet rule. This is a widely accepted theory developed by Linus Pauling; it has great explanatory power, but does not correspond to actual physical processes. The theory predicts that a 2s electron becomes energized, or excited, and is "promoted" to a vacant 2p orbital; then, the half filled 2s orbital and the three half filled 2s orbitals combine to form the hybrid sp3 orbital which can then form bonds with other atoms. The ability of C to form a virtually infinite number of compounds despite its ground state electron configuration of 1s22s22p2 is explained by the orbital hybridization theory. Though C is the most striking application of the theory, N and O can also hybridize.

Properties of C

Carbon is the most significant element in organic chemistry due to its abundance and bonding properties. C tends to form four covalent bonds, either with other C atoms or with other elements, because of its four valence electrons. This tendency is called tetravalency and accounts for the large number and strength of carbon compounds. These properties also explain the possible geometry of C compounds: if all four valence electrons form covalent bonds, the resulting molecule has a tetrahedral shape; this can be visualized as placing bonded atoms around the central C atom at the four corners of a three-dimensional pyramid. C is represented in structural formulas as C surrounded by four single lines on a plane; this structure is merely for convenience—one should always remember that molecules are three dimensional.

Bond dissociation energy

Simply stated, bond dissociation energy is the energy required to break a bond and is represented in equations as $DH°$. This energy can be measured and is useful in calculations involving enthalpy, the measurement of heat energy released or absorbed in a reaction. The bond in question is broken homolytically, meaning that each portion of the now-separated compound has one of the electrons that formed the covalent bond. The general process is represented as follows, where the double dots represent a pair of shared electrons: $X : Y \rightarrow X\cdot + \cdot Y$. In reality, however, the bonds under examination are parts of polyatomic molecules, so the bond dissociation energy is difficult to measure precisely. It increases as the difference in electronegativity between two atoms increases and is thus predictable using the trends on the periodic table.

Coordinate covalent bonds

If one atom in a binary compound or bonded pair provides both electrons for the covalent bond, a coordinate covalent bond results. For instance, when ammonia (NH_3) bonds with boron trifluoride (BF_3), the electron pair in the covalent bond between N and B come only from N. N has five valence electrons, three of which are bonded to H in the ammonia molecule. B has three valence electrons, all of which are bonded to F. The N—B covalent bond, therefore, depends on the two remaining electrons from N. Coordinate covalent bonds are important in a large number of biological processes involving essential metals such as zinc, magnesium, copper, and iron. They can have a large impact on molecular geometry because of the demanding nature of the conditions in which coordinate covalent bonds may be formed.

Bonding capacity of nonmetals

Nonmetals have predictable bonding capacities based on the number of valence electrons in an atom of each element. Because of their electron configurations, nonmetals form molecular compounds with other nonmetals through covalent bonds. Each nonmetal atom tends to form the number of covalent bonds required to meet the octet rule—a number corresponding to the number of single or unpaired electrons in its outer energy level. For example, C contains four valence electrons, so it tends to form four covalent bonds to meet the octet rule; O contains two valence electrons and forms two covalent bonds. The number of covalent bonds a nonmetal atom is likely to form can easily be determined from its dot structure. In the two examples shown here, the dot structure for fluorine shows one unpaired electron, so atomic fluorine will form one covalent bond. Selenium forms two.

```
  ..
: F :

  .


  .
: Se :

  .
```

Bonding capacity of metals

Metals have very small numbers of valence electrons; most have two, and some have one or more than two. In a solid state, metals form strong bonds because their loosely bound electrons become delocalized, or they overlap with electron orbitals of neighboring atoms, much like a covalent bond. A solid metal is therefore a large collection of atoms whose electrons overlap with the orbitals of up to eight neighboring atoms, forming very strong bonds through the electrostatic attraction between positive nuclei and a sea of negative orbiting electrons. These strong bonds result in many of the typical metallic traits such as high melting point, ductile strength, and malleability. The delocalized electrons also account for the conductivity of metals—another characteristic property—because their weak attraction to a central atom means they are free to disperse electrical charges as they move about the solid.

Nonbonding electrons

Nonbonding electrons, also called lone-pair electrons or unshared electron pairs, are those in lower energy levels (non-valence) and those in valence shells not engaged in a bond at any given moment. Though not involved in bonds, they exert influence on the shapes of molecules by their forces of attraction and repulsion. Because they occupy more space than bonded electrons, nonbonded electrons exert greater force on neighboring atoms and molecules and can force the orbitals into closer contact than VSEPR theory would seem to predict, thus changing the geometry of the molecule. Atoms or molecules containing at least one unpaired electron are called free radicals; their lone electrons make them highly reactive and unstable. Nonbonding electrons in lower energy levels can become available for bonding through hybridization.

Diatomic elements

Diatomic elements tend to appear in pairs because of their electron configuration and bonding properties. Some nonmetals have such a strong tendency to form covalent bonds that atoms of a single element bond with one another in their non-molecular state. In other words, when the element is not in a compound, atoms of that element bond to themselves. Two typical examples are Cl and Br, both of which form one covalent bond with their single unpaired electron. Diatomic atoms satisfy the octet rule by sharing their single electron with another atom of the same element, which means that these elements appear as molecules until they react with other substances.

The diatomic molecules are H_2, N_2, O_2, F_2, Cl_2, Br_2, and I_2.

Ionic bonding

The transfer of electrons from one atom to another is called ionic bonding. Atoms that lose or gain electrons are referred to as ions. The gain or loss of electrons will result in an ion having a positive or negative charge. Here is an example: Take an atom of sodium (Na) and an atom of chlorine (Cl). The sodium atom has a total of 11 electrons as well as one electron in its outer shell. The chlorine has 17 electrons as well as 7 electrons in its outer shell. From this, the atomic number, or number of protons, of sodium can be calculated as 11 because the number of protons equals the number of electrons in an atom. When sodium chloride (NaCl) is formed, one electron from sodium transfers to chlorine. Ions have charges. They are written with a plus (+) or minus (-) symbol. Ions in a compound are attracted to each other because they have opposite charges.

Covalent bonds

A covalent bond is formed when two electrons are shared by two atoms. For example, H2 is formed as:

$$H\cdot + \cdot H \longrightarrow H\colon H$$

Each electron in the shared pair is attracted to each of the two nuclei participating in the bond. It is this attraction that holds the hydrogen atoms together and is responsible for covalent bonding in this and other types of molecules. Only valence electrons are involved in the covalent bonding of atoms with many electrons, i.e., atoms other than hydrogen. The octet rule provides a means of accounting for the valence electrons in a molecule. It states that for atoms other than hydrogen, bonds tend to form until the individual atoms are surrounded by eight valence electrons.

Covalent bonding is characterized by the sharing of one or more pairs of electrons between two atoms or between an atom and another covalent bond. This produces an attraction to repulsion stability that holds these molecules together. Atoms have the tendency to share electrons with each other so that all outer electron shells are filled. The resultant bonds are always stronger than the intermolecular hydrogen bond and are similar in strength to ionic bonds. Covalent bonding occurs most frequently between atoms with similar electronegativities. Nonmetals are more likely to form covalent bonds than metals since it is more difficult for nonmetals to liberate an electron, electron sharing takes place when one species encountered another species with similar electronegativity. Covalent bonding of metals is important in both process chemistry and industrial catalysis.

There are two types of covalent bonds: polar and non-polar. Polar bonds in molecules depend on the difference in electronegativity between the individual atoms in the compound and the compounds degree of asymmetry resulting in the unequal sharing of the electrons. A completely polar bond is

- 81 -

more correctly described as an ionic bond and occurs when the difference in the electronegativity between 2 atoms is so great that one atom takes the electron of the other. If the difference in the electronegativity between 2 atoms of a molecule is between 0.4 and 1.7, the bond is polar. Non-polar bonds in molecules occur when the electronegativity of the individual atoms is relatively equal, resulting in the equal sharing of electrons. Most non-polar molecules are hydrophobic at room temperature. The most common form is the hydrogen bond.

The bond order indicates how many pairs of electrons are shared between atoms forming a covalent bond:

- The single bond is the most common type of covalent bond. It shares one pair of electron between two atoms.
- All other bonds with more than one shared pair of electrons are considered multiple covalent bonds.
- The double bond exists when 2 pairs of electrons are shared. An example is ethylene in which the sharing is between the carbon atoms.
- The triple bond exists when three pairs of electrons are shared. An example is hydrogen cyanide in which the sharing is between Carbon and Nitrogen.
- Quadruple bonds exist although they are rare and are mainly found in transition metals.

- Quintuple bonds have been found to exist in some dichromium compounds.
- Sextuple bonds can exist in diatomic dimolybdenum and ditungsten.
- Other bonds that are rarer include molecules with three center bonds.

Valence bonds

The model for valence bonds has been supplemented in recent times with the molecular orbital model. This model illustrates the atoms being brought together and the formation of hybrid molecular orbitals by an interaction with atomic orbitals. The molecular orbitals are a cross between original atomic orbitals and usually will extend between two bonding atoms. Quantum mechanics, which is the modern theory of action that is applied on very small scales, can be used to calculate the electronic structure, bond angles, bond distances and energy levels of simple molecules with great accuracy. Bond distances can be determined with as much accuracy as measurement provides. Energy calculations for small molecules are accurate enough to be used in determining thermodynamic heats of formation.

Molecular geometry

Bond angle, bond length, and conjugation
Bond angle is the angle in degrees between two bonds of the same atom. Imagine axes running from the nuclei of

bonded atoms to the central atom's nucleus. The angle between two such axes is the bond angle. It is a fundamental variable in molecular geometry and is influenced by specific atomic properties such as electronegativity and the number of electrons. Bond length is another fundamental variable; it is the distance between the nuclei of two bonded atoms. It increases with the size of the bonded atoms, and is predictable based on periodic trends. Bond length between atoms of the same element decreases as the number of electrons involved in the bond increases; a double bond is shorter than a single bond, and a triple bond is shorter than a double bond. Conjugation is the alternation of single and double bonds within a compound; the varying bond lengths influence the overall geometry.

Significance to chemistry

The consistent ways in which atoms combine to form compounds enable chemists to predict the shapes, or geometries, of the molecules of any given compound. Knowing the shapes of molecules can in turn allow researchers to better understand the nature of matter such as crystalline structures, the nature of chemical reactions and how to facilitate or impede them to reach a desired outcome, such as in developing new drugs or petroleum refinement technology. On a molecular level, the shape of a molecule can increase or decrease its reactivity because the electrons available for reactions are less accessible to other particles in more complexly shaped molecules. If part of a molecule blocks its

reactive site(s), a reaction is less likely to occur, and sometimes a molecule of a specific shape requires another specific shape to react with it.

VSEPR theory

The Valence Shell Electron Pair Repulsion theory is based on the fact that particles of similar charges repel one another. Electrons surrounding an atom will therefore arrange themselves to be as far apart from one another as possible. Using these laws, VSEPR theory predicts how electron pairs will arrange themselves around a given nucleus, making important predictions about the reactivity and geometry of molecules and atoms. The Lewis structure for barium, :Ba: , shows the electron pairs at their maximum possible separation of 180°. Boron, containing three valence pairs, forms bonds at 120° angles because its electron pairs must be evenly spaced on a 360° plane. All pairs are not equal; bonded pairs of electrons exert less repulsion than nonbonded pairs. VSEPR theory thus predicts an angular shape for H_2O molecules: the nonbonded electrons in O press the H atoms closer together than the 180° one might expect.

Intermolecular forces

Intermolecular forces, also called van der Waals forces for their 19th century Dutch discoverer, are the electrostatic (or ionic) attractions between molecules. Because molecules in gases move so fast and are so far apart, the intermolecular attraction in gases is not an important factor in reactions. These forces are strongest in liquids and solids where they may determine the alignment of the molecules. Dipole interactions occur when the negatively and positively charged poles of molecules are attracted to one another; if the attractions are strong enough, the molecules form loose bonds, with the resulting structure shaped by the way the poles attract one another. Tightly bound molecules form solids, while loosely bound molecules form liquids. Nonpolar intermolecular attractions may occur when the electrons within a molecule are momentarily attracted to the positively charged nucleus of another molecule.

Coulomb force

There are two types of electric charge, positive and negative. When a negative charge has been rubbed off a cat's fur onto one's hands, the cat is left positively charged and the hand negatively charged. At the basis of this is the idea that action at a distance is caused by charges which are the sources of forces. With the electric "Coulomb force" the magnitude is in proportion to the product of the charges and inversely proportional to the square of the distance between them. This vector can be written either:

$$F_x = q_1 q_2 R_x / 4 \prod \varepsilon_0 r^3,$$
or
$$F = q_1 q_2 / 4 \prod \varepsilon r^2.$$

In the equation, q1 and q2 are the charge magnitudes. R is a vector pointing from one to the other and r acts as the distance in between them.

London forces and hydrogen bonding

In nonpolar molecules, electrons are normally distributed evenly throughout their respective electron clouds, or energy levels. But those molecules can become temporarily polarized, having regions in which electrical charges are stronger or weaker than nearby regions. In this polarized state, the molecules are attracted to one another through weak forces called London forces.

The hydrogen bond is the attractive force between an H atom in one molecule and any electronegative atom in another nearby molecule. This bond is very prevalent in nature and is weaker than covalent or ionic bonds, but stronger than other intermolecular forces. Water molecules are highly polar and the H atoms of water molecules are strongly attracted to the O atoms of other water molecules. Similar H bonds are operable in NH3 and HF. These bonds are represented in structural formulas by a series of four dots between H and an electronegative atom of a neighboring molecule.

IUPAC nomenclature and common names

The International Union of Pure and Applied Chemistry developed and recommends a set of conventions and standards for naming chemical compounds. Collectively, these conventions are known as "nomenclature." The aim of using standardized nomenclature is to eliminate ambiguity or confusion over the composition of a given substance under discussion. In the ideal application of the conventions, the correct chemical formula of a substance can be derived from its name and its structure can often be described by proper application of the standards. Nomenclature uses prefixes, suffixes, and infixes to indicate the formula for and, if necessary, the placement of constituent parts within compounds. Many compounds were named before the standardization of nomenclature guidelines and so do not conform to them. Names such as formaldehyde, propane, and methane, for example, do not identify the numbers of C atoms present as IUPAC rules dictate. These are referred to as common names.

Inorganic binary compounds

The standard steps for naming inorganic binary compounds are:

- When a metal is present, name the metal first.
- Name the root of the non-metal, and add the suffix "-ide."
- Examples: sodium chloride, aluminum bromide, potassium sulfide, sodium pentoxide.
- When a metal is not present, the first element to be named is determined by starting at the left of the periodic table; the left-most element is named first. A Greek prefix must indicate the number of the prefixed atom present in the molecule. When only one atom of the first element is present, no prefix is necessary.

- Examples: carbon monoxide, dinitrogen tetrachloride, triphosphorous pentafluoride. Hydrogen dioxide.
- When properly followed, conventions of nomenclature describe the quantities and nature of chemicals in the compounds named.

Acids

Because they form an important class of chemicals, acids have their own slightly different system of nomenclature. Hydrogen-based acids have the prefix "hydro," followed by the root of the halogen, and ending with the suffix "-ic." Thus, HF, "Hydrogen fluoride," is called in solution "Hydrofluoric acid." Other examples include: HCl – hydrochloric acid, HBr – hydrobromic acid, HI – hydroiodic acid. Another class of acids is very abundant in nature: oxygen based acids—oxoacids, or carboxylic acids—contain hydrogen, oxygen, and another element. Many of them have common names, but their IUPAC names are derived by naming the oxoanion, using the suffix "-ic," and adding acid. Thus NO_3^-, a nitrate anion, combines in solution with hydrogen and is called nitric acid—HNO_3. "Sulfate" becomes sulfuric acid; "chlorate" becomes "chloric acid," and so on.

Organic compounds

While the naming of inorganic compounds depends on the type of bonds between molecules, nomenclature for organic compounds is most directly driven by the functional groups present within it. Organic nomenclature describes the bonding between atoms as rings and/or chains, and identifies the type and location of functional groups within the compound. The names of organic compounds will generally have three parts: a root indicating the largest chain or ring structure of the carbon atoms present, a suffix designating the molecule's functional group(s), and names of other groups or elements present. Other rules for organic nomenclature vary depending on the type of hydrocarbon chain forming the parent, or root, and the types of bonds present within that chain. Cyclic hydrocarbons, those formed in rings, also have slight variations in nomenclature conventions applied to them.

In naming organic compounds, the longest carbon chain or ring, also called the parent hydrocarbon, forms the root of the compound name. These roots correspond to the number of C atoms present in the longest chain and are classified into groups such as alkanes, alkenes, and alkynes. Alkenes contain only saturated hydrocarbons in which the C atoms are bound with single bonds. Alkenes are unsaturated chains containing double bonds, and alkynes are unsaturated chains in which the C atoms are joined in triple bonds. Roots may belong to any of these classes as indicated by their suffix. The following are some common parent (or root) names and their corresponding number of C atoms:

Root name	# of C atoms	Root name	# of C atoms
Meth	1	Undec	11
Eth	2	Dodec	12
Prop	3	Tridec	13
But	4	Tetradec	14
Pent	5	Icos	15
Hex	6	Henicos	16
Hept	7	Docos	17
Oct	8	Triacont	18
Non	9	Tetracont	19
Dec	10	Pentacont	20

According to IUPAC nomenclature guidelines, suffixes describe the family group or functional group/groups present in the named compound. Each functional group is associated with a corresponding suffix which is to be attached to the root name of the parent hydrocarbon. Some common functional groups and their suffixes are as follows:

Group	Suffix	Group	Suffix
Alkane	-ane	Ketone	-one
Alkene	-ene	Carboxylic acid	-oic acid
Alkyne	-yne	Alcohol	-ol
Aldehyde	-al	Ether	-ether
Sulfide	-sulfide	Amine	-amine
Ester	-oate	Amide	-amide

A compound including a propanoate, therefore, is formed from an alkane, "prop," parent hydrocarbon ($CH_3CH_2CH_3$) with an ester functional group attached. There are actually two suffixes in propanoate: -ane indicates an alkane (a saturated non-cyclic

- 86 -

hydrocarbon) and –oate indicates an ester.

Names of organic compounds, which can be very complex molecules, use numbers to indicate the location of groups or substituents attached to the carbon chain. To determine these numbers, each C atom or CH molecule in the ring or chain is assigned a number designating its proximity to the highest priority functional group. The example below shows an organic compound with a carboxyl group attached at the far right. The C atoms are numbered starting with 1 at the carboxyl C atom, and moving to the left. Thus the C atom on the far left is the 5th C atom in the parent chain. The IUPAC name indicates that the Br is attached to the 4th C atom and the methyl group (CH3) is attached to the 3rd.

Br   CH₃   O
| | ‖
CH₃—CH—CH—CH₂—C—OH
5   4   3   2   1
4-bromo-3-methylpentanoic acid

Alkanes
Alkanes present unique challenges for nomenclature because of the many isomers (structural variations) possible. The standard IUPAC conventions for organic compounds apply: each name consists of a prefix, a parent (or root), and a suffix. But the names of alkanes further specify the length of the C parent and the position of any alkyl groups (an alkane which has lost an H atom, becoming CH3). The prefix indicates the type and location of alkyl groups, but a new suffix, --yl, indicates the presence of an alkyl. The

simplest alkane, for instance, is methane (CH4); when an H is lost, it becomes methyl (CH3). Alkyl groups are generally represented in structural or condensed structural formulas as R—.

Alkenes
The IUPAC rules for naming alkenes are very similar to those for alkanes, but because the double bond present in the chain is the primary identifying characteristic of an alkene, the location of the bond must be specified. The longest C chain containing the double bond is the parent chain and a Greek prefix identifies the number of C atoms. An alkene with eight carbon atoms is therefore an octene (a chain of eight C atoms with no double bonds is an octane). Counting C atoms from the end of the chain nearer the double bond, the number of the first C in the double bond precedes the parent name, as in 3-octene. Using the same numbering method, the positions of alkyls or other groups in the chain are also identified.

Alkynes and aromatic compounds
The distinguishing characteristic of alkynes is the triple bond; therefore, the nomenclature conventions must identify the presence of the triple bond with the suffix –yne and its location with a prefixed number derived from the same numbering method as with alkenes. 3-octyne therefore indicates a hydrocarbon chain containing a CÐC triple bond which begins at the 3rd C atom from the end. Prefixed numbers also indicate the bond location of alkyl or other substituents groups.

- 87 -

Aromatic compounds are those in which a hydrocarbon ring, called a benzene ring (C_6H_6), is the parent. They are named by adding substituent groups as prefixes, for example: a simple compound in which bromium is attached to a benzene is BrC_6H_6, or bromobenzene; an ethyl group (CH_2CH_3) attached to benzene is called ethylbenzene; NO_2 attached to a benzene is nitrobenzene, and so on.

Esters and ethers

Ethers are commonly named alkyl ethers because of their chemical structure (C—O—C). When other groups or alkyls are present, they are named in alphabetical order followed by "ether," as in butyl methyl ether. Formal IUPAC guidelines, however, dictate that ethers be called alkoxyalkanes in which the smaller alkyl and the O atom form an alkoxy group. The ether, or alkoxy group, is considered a substituent on the longest parent chain or ring. For example, a six carbon alkane is a hexane; if an alkoxy group is attached to the hexane at the fourth carbon atom, the compound is 4-methoxyhexane. For esters, the alkyl group bonded to the O is named first, followed by the parent root with the –ate suffix indicating an ether, as in methyl benzoate ($OCOCH_3$).

Aldehydes and ketones

Familiar aldehydes and ketones have common names such as formaldehyde and acetone, but the IUPAC conventions apply to more complex compounds. Aldehydes are named by identifying the longest C chain containing the C=O bond. Each substituent group is then named, preceded by the number of the C atom to which it is attached; the count of C atoms begins at the C=O bond. The suffix –al identifies the compound as an aldehyde, as in 3-hydroxy-2-methylbutanal. The C=O bond is understood to be on the terminal C atom of the chain. Ketone nomenclature differs in that the C=O bond is not the terminal atom, so it must be numbered in a prefix to the name of the compound. Count the C atoms beginning at the end nearest the double bond. A suffix –one indicates a ketone, as in 4-methyl-2-pentanone.

Pauling scale

Acclaimed chemist Linus Pauling developed the Pauling scale in 1932. On the scale, an electronegative value of 3.98 is given to the most common electronegative chemical element, which is fluorine. Texts may often use the value 4.0. The least electronegative element, which is francium, has a value of 0.7. The rest of the elements have values that are in between these. Hydrogen is arbitrarily given a value of 2.1 or 2.2 on the Pauling scale. Bonds between atoms with a large electronegative difference, those more than or equal to 1.7, are normally considered to be ionic. Those with values between 1.7 and 0.4 are normally thought of as polar covalent. Those with values below 0.4 are non-polar covalent bonds. An electronegativity difference of 0 indicates a covalent bond that is entirely non-polar.

Organic chemistry and biochemistry

Organic chemistry is the study of organic chemicals, all of which contain carbon. These compounds are usually associated with plants, animals, and other life forms; while inorganic compounds are associated with minerals and do not usually contain carbon. Biochemistry seeks to understand the mostly organic compounds involved in life processes and how they interact and change to support life functions. 99% of the compounds necessary for life are organic, but some are mineral atoms, such as phosphorus, potassium, iron, chlorine, magnesium, and calcium. Biochemistry, therefore, encapsulates organic chemistry, but an organic chemist need not know a great deal about biochemistry. Many millions of compounds are studied and described by these two sub fields of chemistry.

$$\begin{array}{c} O \\ \| \\ -C-H \end{array}$$
Aldehyde

$$\begin{array}{c} O \\ \| \\ -C- \end{array}$$
Ketone

Carbohydrates

Carbohydrates are important organic molecules containing carbon, hydrogen, and oxygen; they are the primary source of energy for most living organisms. Carbohydrate digestion is the result of several fundamental metabolic pathways and each process involves a great many subsidiary reactions. The formation of glucose from carbohydrates is one important pathway. Glucose ($C_6H_{12}O_6$) is one of several monosaccharides produced from carbohydrates by chemical reactions. Glucose molecules then enter another metabolic pathway called glycolysis in which they are broken down into pyruvate ($C_3H_4O_3$), which in turn begins another series of cascading reactions which lead to usable energy. The citric acid cycle is another important metabolic pathway in the digestion of carbohydrates.

Lipids

Lipids are bimolecular that are insoluble in water but soluble in other nonpolar solvents. They are responsible for the waxy or greasy nature of substances found in plants and animals. Saponification is a process used to further distinguish classes of lipids; it is the process by which esters are hydrolyzed in base solution to yield glycerol and the salts of fatty acids. If lipids do not contain esters, they are nonsaponifiable and are classified accordingly. Hydrolysis is another important reaction for lipids. In the presence of water and an acid catalyst, lipids break down into glycerol and fatty acids. Hydrogenation is the process of converting C=H double bonds to C—H single bonds resulting in increased saturation of the hydrocarbon and a correspondingly higher melting point.

Proteins

Proteins can also be metabolized for use as a source of energy, but this is merely one catabolic pathway associated with them. Because proteins are constructed of long chains of amino acids, reactions early in the process are of particular interest. One is the oxidation of cysteine, a sulfur-containing amino acid. Two cysteine molecules combine with oxygen and fuse to form an S—S disulfide bond, creating one molecule of cystine. This reaction is important in determining the unique structure of some proteins. Peptides are groups of two or more linked amino acids. Peptide formation occurs during protein synthesis when a carboxyl group reacts with an amine of a second amino acid to release water and form an amide bond which links the two amino acids into a peptide. The amide bond is called a peptide bond; many such reactions can produce long chains (polypeptides) that eventually become proteins.

Protein hydrolysis and denaturation

Protein hydrolysis is one of the processes within the metabolic pathway that produces energy for use by living cells. Proteins may be hydrolyzed by acids or bases or by water due to its highly polar molecules. Long protein chains are broken into smaller peptides and, with increased time, temperature, or acidity/basicity, the peptides can be reduced to individual amino acids. Hydrolysis reactions in digestion are catalyzed by enzymes present in animals' digestive systems. Denaturation is the process by which the orderly structure of natural proteins is broken through exposure to conditions such as high temperatures and certain compounds. The protein's folds and helical structures straighten and twist into random forms, making the protein inactive. Denaturation of toxic proteins explains why boiling water to kill bacteria makes it safe to drink—the bacteria no longer produce harmful proteins and the present proteins become denatured.

Protein synthesis

One of the most fundamental processes for life, protein synthesis, is a complex series of reactions involving large compounds. The synthesis occurs at the surface of ribosomal RNA (rRNA) particles suspended in the cytoplasm of cells. Amino acids bonded to transfer RNA (tRNA) are brought to the sites and the translation of codons into a sequence of amino acids begins if the required compounds are present. If all requirements are met, a series of enzyme-catalyzed steps begins to form long peptide chains. The process begins with the initiation step and concludes with termination, at which point the protein is separated from the rRNA. Most proteins are not yet in the form needed by the cell and are modified by more complex reactions to produce the needed protein.

Enzymes

Some of the most important functions associated with enzymes regulate their activity. Enzymes can exist in an inactive or preactive state called zymogens or proenzymes. They are stored until needed by a cell for a specific reaction and are then released and activated to become active enzymes. They are activated by breaking one or more peptide bonds on the enzyme through hydrolysis reactions. Enzyme activity is also regulated by substances called modulators which bond to the enzyme and change its three dimensional orientation, rendering it temporarily inactive. Modulators can be either activators, which increase the enzyme's activity, or inhibitors, which decrease it. Some substances act as uncontrollable, irreversible inhibitors and are thus highly toxic. Cyanide and other heavy metals are deadly because of their inhibitory functions. Enzyme inhibition is a process in which products at the end of reactions inhibit earlier reaction steps, effectively regulating the concentration of target compounds.

Enzymes are catalysts in metabolic pathways and play roles in very large numbers of reactions; all of them are globular proteins and catalyze reactions involving other proteins, making them of fundamental importance in complex bioprocesses. Most enzymes are highly selective, catalyzing only specific reactions when the reactants come into contact with the reactive site of the much larger enzyme molecule. For instance, the enzyme urease is a catalyst in only one reaction: the hydrolysis of urea. By contrast, other catalysts, such as strong acids or bases, catalyze they hydrolysis of any amide. Enzymes are complex proteins that are highly catalytic, increasing the rate of some reactions by as much as 10^{20} times. Enzymes are named systematically with a set of conventions much like IUPAC nomenclature. These conventions specify the reactant and functional group acted upon and the type of reaction catalyzed. A suffix –ase indicates the named compound is an enzyme.

Nucleic acids

Nucleic acids are polymers composed of many smaller nucleotides which can be further broken down to phosphoric acid, organic bases, amines, and deoxyribose or ribose. The nucleotides link to form the polymers in an alternating sequence of phosphate units and sugar units. A nucleic acid containing deoxyribose as its sugar is deoxyribonucleic acid, or DNA. If ribose is the sugar, the compound is ribonucleic acid, or RNA. Nucleic acids are important substances in biochemistry; DNA is the fundamental constituent of genes carrying hereditary information and occurs in a complex molecular arrangement known as the double helix. RNA is a compound essential to the proper formation and utilization of proteins within cells and is found in several varieties including the most common tRNA (transfer RNA) and mRNA (messenger RNA).

Codons

Codons are long molecules formed of nucleotides and found in mRNA. Each codon is specific to the protein in whose synthesis it plays a lead role; each one has unique properties such as molecular weight. Codons are long because they contain three nucleotides for each amino acid required by their target protein. They are attached to ribosomes, which can move through several codons of the mRNA during protein synthesis. The ribosome chemically activates the appropriate codon to form amino acids in proper sequence for the necessary protein. It is a codon which eventually signals the completion of the protein and the separation of the peptide chain from the ribosome.

Carbon

Organic chemistry is to a large degree dependent on the properties of carbon. All organic compounds contain C (although some inorganic compounds also contain C); this is the basis of all life on Earth. The primary property of C responsible for its importance is its ability to form very stable covalent bonds with other C atoms or with other elements. It has four valence electrons, making it an important partner with other atoms according to the octet rule. Another important characteristic of C is its ability to form many different isomers in compounds with other elements, particularly H and the functional groups. Finally, C is important because of its tendency to hybridize, or mix s and p orbitals to form a sp3 hybrid orbital. Carbon's electron configuration by itself does not adequately explain its tetravalent bonding ability; hybridization is necessary to explain it.

Primary, secondary, and tertiary carbon
Primary, secondary, and tertiary carbon atoms are those in a structure or molecule bonded to only one, two, or three other C atoms, respectively. These terms are useful for the specification of C atoms in organic compounds. Because C is involved in so many complex molecules, it is important to be able to distinguish one C atom from another; these designations are one way of doing so. Knowing which type of C atom is under consideration can give clues about its position in a chain or ring. A primary C, for instance, may be the end of a hydrocarbon chain and may have other atoms or groups of atoms attached; a primary carbon may also be part of a double or triple bond (i.e., an alkene or alkyne).

Carbocation, carbanion, carbene, and carbenium ion
Because of Carbon's foundational importance to nomenclature and organic chemistry in general, names were devised to specify slight variations in the structure and charge of C atoms when bonded under circumstances which give them unique characteristics. A carbocation is a positively charged C ion; they occur under various circumstances and may be part of much larger molecules. A carbanion is a negatively charged C ion which features an unshared electron pair on a carbon atom, such as H_3C-. Carbene is a general name for any molecule $H_2C:$, or molecules formed from substitution reactions within that configuration. The molecule is electrically neutral and contains a nonbonding electron pair on the C atom. Carbenium ions are carbocations having at least one structure attached which contains a C

atom with a vacant p orbital and hence a slight positive charge.

Hydrocarbons

Hydrocarbons are molecules containing only C and H and form the basis of organic chemistry. They bond together with strong covalent bonds in chains or rings to form the backbone of organic molecules which may have any number of a large variety of functional groups attached. Hydrocarbons are classified into two large groups based on the bonds between their C atoms; if only C—C single bonds are present, the hydrocarbon is saturated because other electrons will then form bonds with surrounding H atoms. If the C atoms are bound with multiple bonds (C=C or CÐC), fewer electrons are available to form bonds with H atoms and the hydrocarbon is unsaturated. Hydrocarbons are very stable molecules because of the tetravalency of C; it has four valence electrons making its octet requirement easy to satisfy, which results in very strong bonds.

Organic compounds

There are approximately 9 million known organic compounds, each with its own chemical and physical properties. Listing them all and attempting to classify them by their properties would thus be a meaninglessly complex endeavor. But organic compounds are known to be composed of a hydrocarbon backbone and one or more functional groups attached to the hydrocarbon framework. The functional groups are the basis for organic nomenclature and have characteristic traits and predictable reaction behavior which strongly influence the molecule to which they are attached. Separating the backbone from the functional groups provides a more manageable way to classify large molecules in large numbers because the molecule behaves and reacts according to its functional group since they are the sites of reactions in organic molecules.

Classes

Heterocyclic compounds are organic compounds in which one or more atoms other than C have combined with C to form a ring structure. Parent hydrocarbons may form rings and are then named by adding "cyclo" as a prefix as in cycloalkane and cycloalkene. These are usually the result of substitution reactions; for example, a N atom takes the place of a C atom in a cycloalkane. Aromatic compounds are those whose parent is a benzene ring—a cyclic C compound containing 6 C atoms. Aliphatic compounds are those whose parent hydrocarbons take the form of a chain. Biomolecules are large, complex organic molecules that are essential to biological processes; examples are lipids, carbohydrates, enzymes, proteins, etc.

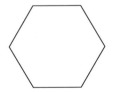

Physical properties

Organic compounds are usually covalently bonded (though specific molecules may be polarized) and, therefore, are less soluble in water than inorganic compounds whose ionic bonds are easily separated by polarized water molecules. The intramolecular forces in organic molecules are relatively weak compared to the same forces in inorganic compounds; this is also due to the prevalence of covalent bonds. Organic compounds' melting and boiling points are below 300° C, while inorganic melting and boiling points can be much higher. They react more readily with oxygen in combustion (though activation energy is required) and are poor conductors of electrical current. They occur in nature more frequently in gaseous and liquid states, or as solids with low melting points. Inorganic compounds, by contrast, more often appear as solids with high melting points.

Stoichiometry

Stoichiometry is the method by which the mass of compounds and how those various masses interact during reactions can be calculated. The law of conservation of mass states that no detectable quantities of mass are lost in a reaction. For example, if a candle is burned in a sealed jar, the mass of the jar and its contents will be the same before burning the candle as after. Stoichiometric calculations, therefore, are important in describing how elements in a compound relate to one another and in predicting the chemical properties of products of reactions. These calculations have practical application in many industrial functions. For instance, they allow manufacturers of ammonia to know how much raw materials (methane, water, and air) are necessary to produce a desired amount of ammonia.

Mole

The mole is a unit of measurement for the number of particles in an amount of matter. A mole contains the same number of particles as is present in exactly 12 grams of carbon-12, or Avogadro's number, 6.0221415×10^{23}. The particles counted must be specified, and may be atoms, molecules, electrons, or other particles. For example, a mol of water may be said to contain either a mol of H_2O molecules, or three moles of atoms. The mole is significant because it allows different substances with widely varying density and mass to be measured in consistent and comparable ways, enabling predictions and calculations important to chemical reactions and their products. Molar mass is an important number calculated using the mole; it is the number of grams per mole of a given element or compound.

Variations in usage

Because a mole is a unit of measurement for different types of particles, the term is used differently depending on the units being measured. At its most basic meaning, a "mole of an element" is the amount of that element containing the same number of atoms as 12g of Carbon-12. A "mole of a compound" is the

- 94 -

amount of a compound containing Avogadro's number of formula units. A formula unit is the smallest repeating constituent of a compound expressed in its simplest ratio. For example, NaCl is the simplest ratio (1:1) of sodium to chlorine atoms in table salt, so a mole of the compound contains Avogadro's number of NaCl. Similarly, the molar mass of an element is the number of grams per mole of an element, while the molar mass of a compound is the number of grams per mole of a compound.

Calculations

The mole is the number of particles in a given amount of substance and is the foundation of many important calculations. These include the following:

- Changing moles to grams gives the weight in grams of a mole of any substance.
- Changing grams to moles is a calculation giving the number of moles present in a substance when its weight in grams is known.
- When the number of moles is known, the number of particles in a substance can be calculated using Avogadro's number.
- Molar mass calculations give the mass of a given substance per number of moles.

These calculations are important in chemistry because they allow precise measurement of substances present and provide mathematically reliable constants for very large numbers of particles. Considering Avogadro's number of

particles (6.0221415×10^{23}) at a time, rather than a single particle, is a powerful element of stoichiometry and all chemical equations.

Mole, molar mass, and Avogadro's number

The amount of a substance that contains as many elementary units (atoms, molecules, etc.) as there are atoms in exactly 12 grams of carbon, 12 is defined in the SI system of units as a mole. The number of units is determined experimentally and the currently accepted value is

1 mole = 6.022×10^{23} units

This number is called Avogadro's number and it is named in honor of Italian scientist Amedeo Avogadro. The molar mass of an element is the mass in grams or kilograms of 1 mole of the element, or 6.022×10^{23} atoms of the element. For all the elements, the molar mass is equal to its atomic mass in atomic mass units.

Volumetric analysis

Volumetric analysis is simply a system of measurement revolving around volume rather than mass. It is used to determine the volume of a given substance which is an unknown portion of another substance; titration is a form of volumetric analysis. Normality is a unit of measurement designed to simplify and speed up the process of volumetric analysis. It is represented in equations as N (but don't confuse it with the chemical symbol for Nitrogen!). The unit is the molarity of a solution expressed in dissociable H or OH ions. For example, a 1 M solution of HCl contains 1 mol/L of reactable H atoms, and so is 1.0 N (signifying normality); it could also be stated as 1 "equivalent" per liter, referring to the value's comparison relative to the reactable H.

Structural formulas

<u>Conventions and uses</u>
Structural formulas represent the bonds within a molecule using simple lines to show which atoms are bound together. The number of lines connecting elements shows the number of pairs of electrons shared between the two atoms. Ranging from quite simple to very complex, structural formulas can be used to represent the ring and chain structures often present in organic molecules. A structural formula for $C_2H_6O_2$ is shown here. Each line indicates a molecular bond between atoms formed by sharing one pair of electrons. Carbon atoms in compounds often share two pairs (though not in this example), which would be indicated by a double line between the C atoms.

<u>Condensed structural formulas</u>
Because structural formulas can be unwieldy and awkward to write, especially for large molecules, condensed structural formulas were developed as a way to represent the same information in an easier-to-use format. As in structural formulas, condensed structural formulas describe the bonds between atoms and the numbers of atoms present. Unlike structural formulas, however, their condensed cousins do not show all the bonds in a molecule; they instead show the bonding sequence reading the structural formula from left to right. For example, $OHC_2H_2C_2H_2HO$ is the condensed structural formula for the compound illustrated in the structural formula definition.

Chemical formulas

Chemical formulas are chemistry's "shorthand." Composed of letters and subscript numbers, they concisely describe the atomic makeup of compounds. The letters are the periodic symbols for each element, and the numbers indicate the number of atoms present of each element. If only one atom is present, no number is needed. A formula is said to be empirical when its subscripts represent the simplest whole number ratio of atoms. For example, H_2O, the empirical formula for water, shows that two atoms of Hydrogen are present for every atom of Oxygen. A molecular formula describes the molecular structure in greater detail, but not necessarily the simplest ratio. For example, benzene's empirical formula is CH reflecting a 1:1 ratio, but the molecule actually contains 6 atoms of each element. The molecular formula is thus C_6H_6. Any compound can be represented with a formula using these conventions. Formulas are pronounced by stating each letter and number individually.

Solutions

Types

Polar and nonpolar solutes and solvents combine in four different ways to form solutions with varying properties. Here are the four possible combinations: polar solute + non polar solvent; polar solute + polar solvent; nonpolar solute + nonpolar solvent; nonpolar solute + polar solvent. Following the "like dissolves like rule," nonpolar solvents dissolve nonpolar solutes in part because little energy is required to separate the weak London forces governing the interaction of nonpolar substances. Polar substances interact through both London forces and dipole-dipole forces, so they require much larger amounts of energy to separate, or to enter into solution. However, for the same reason, they also make very stable solutions, requiring energy to return to separate solute and solvent states. Solutions of unalike molecules require a great deal of energy (they are endothermic) because the dissimilar molecules repel one another, making solutions unlikely to form.

Ideal solutions

An ideal solution is one in which all molecules, whether solvent or solute, interact in the same way. That is, all attractive forces between molecules in such a solution are equal, so the net enthalpy, or change in energy or heat, is zero. Ideal solutions are useful as calibrators for calculated values in colligative properties; because the enthalpy is zero, theoretical calculations of properties such as osmotic pressure or

changes in boiling point can be experimentally confirmed and/or adjusted by comparing them to the known values of ideal solutions. Another way to think of them is that they always follow Raoult's Law exactly, but they are largely mathematical substances—solutions behave in ideal ways only in very dilute forms and are easily subject to change.

Solvation

Solvation is the technical name for the action of dissolving. When a solute mixes uniformly with a solvent so that the two interact on molecular level, this is solvation. Solvation occurs when intermolecular attractions between solvent and solute are greater than the forces holding either the solute or solvent together. The process can be either exothermic or endothermic. The process of dissolving table salt in water is a common example. $H^+_2O^-$ and Na^+Cl^- molecules are highly polar due to their chemical properties—specific regions of the molecules have electrical charges. When $NaCl$ is added to water, the polar H_2O molecules are immediately attracted to the opposite poles of the $NaCl$ molecules. Because this attraction is stronger than those holding the $NaCl$ in a crystal lattice, the Na and Cl ions break apart and move into solution—the salt is "dissolved."

Colligative properties and the "like dissolves like" rule

Colligative properties are physical properties of a substance that are influenced by the concentration of a solution. For example, pure methane, C_6H_6, boils at a given temperature under known atmospheric pressure. If a solute is added to the methane, the boiling point will no longer remain constant. The colligative properties are: vapor pressure reduction, boiling point elevation, freezing point depression, and osmotic pressure.

Like dissolves like refers to the fact that a solvent must be similar in polarity to a solute if the solute is going to dissolve. Salt dissolves easily in water because both are polar substances. Water does not dissolve oil because the lipids and other hydrocarbons of oily substances are not polar. Gasoline, a nonpolar solvent, dissolves nonpolar molecules such as oil and grease.

Measurement of concentration

Solutions can be measured in everyday applications in terms of percentages. For example, a label on a vinegar bottle that says 5% solution means that 5% of the total solution is acetic acid. Concentrations are also measured by mass; HCl purchased for laboratory uses, for example, is usually 37% by mass, meaning that for every 100g of solution, 37g of HCl are present. Parts per million is another term of measurement for very dilute solutions. For more precise concentration measurements, chemists calculate mole fractions, molarity, and molality. Molarity, represented in equations by M, is the number of moles of solute per liter of solution. Molality, represented in equations by m, is the number of moles of solute per kilogram of solvent.

$$M = \frac{moles\, A}{liters\, of\, solution}$$

$$m = \frac{moles\ A}{kg\ of\ solution}$$

Henry's Law

Henry's law defines a constant used in solution equations. It states that the amount of a gas dissolved in a liquid at given temperatures and concentrations corresponds directly to the partial pressure of the gas over the liquid. Or in other words, it states that the volume of a gas that is soluble is proportional to the partial pressure of that gas above the solution in a closed system. Partial pressure is defined as the pressure of a gas if it occupied a container all on its own. It is calculated as $P=kC$, where k is the Henry's law constant, C is the concentration of the gas in moles per liter, and P is the partial pressure. Henry's law is one of the gas laws describing the thermodynamic interaction of temperature, pressure, and volume in gases. The law establishes constants at 25° C.; because pressures change as temperatures change, temperature must be considered when using Henry's Law.

Non water-based inorganic solvents

For much of chemistry's early history, water was the only known solvent. Others gradually came to be used, but usually in aqueous solution. Later developments demanded non-aqueous solvents to study particular reactions that cannot occur in water. Many non aqueous solvents are organic compounds, but some common ones, such as liquid ammonia and sulfur dioxide, are not. In addition to research uses, these types of solvents are significant in many industrial processes. Acids and bases often behave differently in such solvents than in water or water-based solutions. For this reason, it is important to consider the active ions when measuring acidity and basicity of substances in inorganic non aqueous solutions.

Factors affecting solubility

The most obvious factors which influence solubility are temperature and pressure. An increase in solvent temperature increases the solubility of the solid solute—the higher the temperature, the more solute can be dissolved in solution. The impact on temperature is not uniform across substances, and there are a few examples of solvents whose solubility *decreases* with increase in temperature, but these are rare. Gaseous solutes, however, become less soluble at higher temperatures. Pressure impacts solubility only when solvents are in the gaseous state. Much like a system in equilibrium, gaseous solvents move out of solution and back into it under sufficient atmospheric pressure. If atmospheric pressure is not strong enough to force molecules back into solution, the gas escapes into the air—all gaseous solutes will eventually leave solution in an open container.

Conductivity as a physical property of solutions

Pure solvents containing no free ions have very low electrical conductivity; most water has high conductivity because it is not pure H2O—it is a solution containing salts and other minerals whose ions conduct the electrical current. Like the colligative properties, conductivity is influenced by the concentration of solute within a solution. Therefore, water with a lot of table salt (Na^+Cl^-) dissolved in it (a solution) has much greater electrical conductivity than distilled water, which has been processed to remove most substances other than water molecules. However, even the purest water produced in a lab has some conductivity because of the slight tendency (approximately 1 in 50 million) of its H atoms to dissociate and form ions.

Energy in solutions

Although solutions may appear inert and static, they require constant and significant exchanges of and fluctuations in energy. Energy is required at each step of the solvation process, which may be simplified as follows: 1) Solute molecules held together by intermolecular forces must separate; 2) Solvent molecules must also separate to create "room" for the solute; 3) Solvent and solute molecules interact and bond through intermolecular forces. Steps one and two are endothermic, taking energy from outside the system. Step three is slightly exothermic—the energy released is very small. The sum of the changes in heat energy, or enthalpy, for each step is called the heat of solution ($\Delta H°_{sln.}$), and may be either negative (net exothermic) or positive (net endothermic). When it is negative, the intermolecular attraction between molecules in solution is stronger than the attraction between separate solute molecules.

Precipitation reactions

In terms of solutions, precipitation occurs when a solid precipitates out of solution. In typical precipitation reactions, ionic solutes first exist in equilibrium in separate solutions. When the solutions are combined, the ions combine into an insoluble solid which then drops out of solution. The reactions are often quite dramatic, producing bright colors from the mixture of two clear solutions. Consider the following example of a precipitation reaction involving silver nitrate and table salt in separate solutions: $AgNO_3 + NaCl \rightarrow AgCl + NaNO_3$. The solid, silver chloride, is insoluble in water and forms because the intermolecular attraction between Ag+ and Cl- is stronger than that which holds NaCl together. The solid then drops out of solution, appearing as a gray cloud spreading throughout the solution. The reaction may also be expressed as a net ionic equation: $Ag+(aq) + Cl-(aq) \rightarrow AgCl(s)$.

Vapor-pressure reduction and Raoult's Law

When a solute is added to a solvent, the vapor pressure of the resulting solution will be lower than that of the pure solvent. This reduction in vapor pressure is caused by molecules and larger particles of solvent at the surface of the solution, where particles of solvent can escape, i.e., where the solvent can be vaporized. Because of the presence of solute particles, fewer particles of liquid solvent can escape into vapor—the solute particles literally get in the way. Raoult's law, named for the first chemist to investigate the mathematical relationship of vapor pressure to solute concentration, states that the vapor pressure of solution is equal to the vapor pressure of pure solvent times the solute concentration expressed in mole fractions. The equation is as follows: $P_A = P°_A X_A$, where P° is the vapor pressure of the solvent and X is the mole fraction of the solvent.

Boiling point elevation and electrolytic solutes

Substances boil when their vapor pressure—the tendency of liquids or solids to enter gaseous states—equals the atmospheric pressure pressing upon them. When electrolytic solutes—substances that separate in solution into ions—are present in a solution, the boiling point increases because the vapor pressure has been reduced per Raoult's law. Higher temperatures are therefore required to produce sufficient energy to allow particles to escape from solution to vapor. Non electrolytic solutes do not have the same influence on boiling point because they release fewer particles into solution upon solvation. Table sugar, for instance, releases smaller particles into solution when it dissolves, with the smallest possible unit being a single sucrose molecule. However, electrolytic solutes release more particles because molecules are broken apart into individual ions. This number or particles must be considered when calculating the effect of solutes on boiling point.

Freezing point depression and electrolytic solutes

In converse fashion, the addition of electrolytic solutes results in a solution with a lower freezing point than the pure solvent. The additional particles make it more difficult for the liquid solution's molecules to align themselves in a crystal lattice; they require a lower temperature to do so. Water containing large amounts of dissolved salt can thus be cooled below its normal freezing point of 0° C. As with boiling point elevation, the mathematical calculation of freezing point depression depends on the number of particles released during solvation. Electrolytic solutes break apart into individual ions, while non electrolytic solutes can only be reduced to individual molecules. Most organic solutes are non electrolytic so have a much smaller effect on colligative properties than inorganic compounds such as salts.

Osmotic pressure

Osmotic pressure is the pressure exerted by a solvent passing through a membrane in osmosis. It is an important measurement used to predict the concentration of solute required to establish equilibrium on each side of the membrane. Imagine two different concentrations of solution are separated in a closed system by a permeable membrane; water can pass through the membrane, but solute particles do so at a much lower rate. Water will flow from the side with lower concentration to the side with higher concentration, but the greater number of solute particles on the higher concentration side reduce the number of solute particles that are able to pass to the lower side. Because water flows freely through the membrane and solute particles less so, the osmotic pressure on the high concentration side increases, causing water to flow back through the membrane to the lower side until equilibrium is established.

Dielectric constant

The dielectric constant is a measurement of a solvent's ability to dissolve polar substances; it is symbolized in equations by ε. The higher the dielectric constant, the more likely a solvent is to dissolve polar solutes; such solvents are usually highly polar themselves. The value is derived experimentally and is more accurately a reflection of the interaction between solvent and solute rather than a property inherent in the solvent. Water's ε is very high, 78.5, while hexane has a very low dielectric constant of 1.89. Hexane will therefore not dissolve ionic compounds. Other common solvents and their ε are as follows: benzene, 2; diethyl ether, 4; tetrahydrofuran, 7; acetone, 21; ethanol, 24; methanol, 33; dimethyl sulfoxide, 49; and water, 78.5.

Aprotic solvent, amphiprotic solvent, agua regia, and autoprotolysis

Aprotic solvents are those having neither acidic nor basic properties, e.g. having no dissociable H atoms. Pentane and toluene are aprotic solvents. By contrast, amphiprotic solvents exhibit both acidic and basic properties because they have dissociable H atoms. This term is synonymous with amphoteric and ampholytic. Water, ammonia, and ethanol are examples of amphiprotic solvents. Aqua regia is a mixture of nitric acid and hydrochloric acid used in industrial applications such as the dissolution of gold. Autoprotolysis refers to the transfer, or dissociation and reassociation, of H atoms within the same substance. The autoionization of water is a typical example; H and O atoms in water molecules separate to form H^+ and OH^- ions, and then rejoin in the H_2O molecular form. This autoprotolysis exists in equilibrium: H_2O (l) Ý $H^+(aq)$ + $OH^-(aq)$

[OH-], pH, and pOH

OH^- is the hydroxide ion associated with acids. Placing it in square brackets indicates a number of OH^- ions as a variable in equations. pH refers to the "power of Hydrogen" ions concentrated in solution; it is a measurement of the acidity or alkalinity of solution and ranges from 0 to 14. Neutral solutions have a pH of 7; solutions become more acidic as their pH decreases from 7 and more basic as their pH increases from 7. pH is derived as the logarithm of the concentration of H ions: pH = $-\log[H^+]$ In this example, the value of $[H+] = 1.0 \times 10^{-7}$: pH = $-\log[H^+]$ = $-\log(1.0 \times 10^{-7})$ = 5.27, an acidic solution. pOH, the "power of hydroxide ion" is another measurement of concentration in solutions. It is closely related to pH, as is the equation for calculating it: pOH = $-\log[OH^-]$.

Common-ion effect

The common-ion effect describes the impact of adding substances to solution that have ions in common with the solute or solvent. Imagine a solution, H_2O + NaCl, in equilibrium. Adding more salt or more water to the solution causes the equilibrium to shift because the added material has ions in common with the solution. The common-ion effect allows predictions about pH because of the known and quantifiable impacts of changes in solution equilibria. Another solution in equilibrium is shown below:

$HC_2H_3O_2(aq)$Ý$H^+(aq)$ + $C_2H_3O_2^-(aq)$

If we add iron acetate ($FeC_2H_3O_2$) to the solution, we can see that the iron and acetate will separate to form the ions Fe^+ and $C_2H_3O_2^-$. Because the number of acetate ions in the solution will have increased, the equilibrium will shift to the left and establish a new equilibrium as predicted by Le Châtelier's principle.

- 102 -

Titration

Titration is the process by which the amount of a given substance present in solution is determined. If a solution contains an unknown amount of acid, for instance, titration calculations can determine the unknown value by measuring the moles of base required to completely neutralize the acid. Titration can also work in reverse: the unknown quantity of a base in solution is found by adding measured amounts of acid until the base is neutralized. The substance whose amount is unknown is "being titrated;" the substance added in known amounts is the "titrant." In addition to determining concentration, titration can also determine K_a and K_b by slightly modifying the calculations. Titration is typically shown on a titration curve; important changes in the angle of the curve correspond to changes in pH and when neutralization has been achieved, a point called the equivalence point, the pH of the solution will be 7 in the titration of strong acids with strong bases.

Acid-base indicator and acid dissociation constant

Acid-base indicators are substances—often in solution—which indicate changes in pH by changes in color. They are themselves weak acids.

The acid dissociation constant, K_a in equations, is also known as the acid ionization constant. It is a value expressing the point at which an acid dissociation reaction is at equilibrium. In other words, it measures the amount of acid that will break into H^+ and an anion before those ions begin to recombine into their parent molecular form. For instance, acetic acid dissociates as follows: $HC_2H_3O_2(aq) Ý H^+(aq) + C_2H_3O_2^-(aq)$. The equilibrium constant of this equilibrium reaction may be determined by the following equation where square brackets indicate numbers of particles:

$$K_a = \frac{[H^+][C_2H_3O_2^-](aq)}{[HC_2H_3O_2]}$$

This equation is the specific application of a general formula for calculating the value of K_a (below). The formula dictates that the greater the value of HA, the greater the dissociation (or strength) of the acid and the value of K_a.

$$K_a = \frac{[H^+][A^-]}{[HA]}$$

Base constant and water ionization constant

In addition to the acid dissociation constant (K_a) discussed above, the base and water ionization constants are some of the most important constants in acid-base and solution chemistry. The capital letter K is the chemistry symbol for equilibrium constant and the superscript indicates which constant is being measured. K_b, the base ionization (or dissociation) constant, measures a base's strength in reaction with hydronium ions to form the conjugate acid of the base. The value of K_b is inversely related to basicity: the higher the value, the weaker the base.

The water ionization constant, K_w, is the foundation of all equilibrium constants because other constants are measured in comparison to water. Because so few of the H atoms in pure H_2O dissociate, K_w is so small (10-14) as to be virtually zero. This provides a known and reliable baseline against which to measure other constants and equilibria.

Science

Science is a method of acquiring and obtaining knowledge. It is the process of gaining reliable information about the real world, including the explanation of phenomena. It is the development of a body of knowledge about observable phenomena, using the best capabilities humans have at their disposal. The process of organizing and classifying knowledge, through objective observation and evaluation, is a major goal of science. Science can be considered reliable, but it is not infallible. The limits of human knowledge are constantly growing, often making yesterday's science obsolete and simplistic. Science is thus never fixed; it is always subject to change as new information is gained and synthesized with existing knowledge. Ultimately, science is the sum total of knowledge in any period of time, based on the current abilities of man to understand the world of phenomena, verifiable by observable data.

Basic science and applied science

Basic science and applied science share many attributes but are generally motivated by different influences:

- *Basic science* is spurred on by scientific inquiry, the human need to explain the observed physical world. It may have no specific goal, but is man's response to questions that arise from human curiosity and interest. It is usually an attempt to explain the laws of nature by using the scientific method.
- *Applied science* has a specific practical goal or application: It is designed to solve a problem. Industry and government are institutions that use applied science regularly.

Thus, basic and applied science share many qualities, including scientific inquiry and the scientific method. The goals of each can be very different. It should be pointed out that basic science very often provides results that have uses in applied science.

Although basic science may have no stated goal or target, it provides many benefits to society:

- Basic science contributes greatly to human understanding and culture, enriching society in many ways.
- Basic science has been responsible for major breakthroughs that have great social and economic impact.

- Basic science provides derivative solutions that can be used in applied science. For example, basic science was critical to the development of the space program, from which countless valuable applications have been derived.
- Basic science contributes to education and research across the broad spectrum of society.

Scientific method

The steps of the *scientific method* are as follows:

1. The scientific method begins with, and absolutely depends upon, the observation of objective, unbiased data. Any prejudice or bias in the observed data nullifies its validity. Thus the basic input from the observations must be rigorously screened to ensure objectivity.

2. The development of a theory or hypotheses based on objective data is the next step in the scientific method. These theories or hypotheses pose logical expectations that the experiment may yield.

3. Construction of a rigorous and valid experimental method designed to test the theories is the next phase of the scientific method. This experimental method must be carefully constructed to give objective, unbiased conclusions based on the hypotheses posited.

4. Careful and statistically correct analysis and evaluation of the experimental results make up the next stage.

5. Modification and replication of the experiment must then follow to provide a statistically accurate demonstration of the validity of the hypotheses. Equivalent results must be shown from a number of repetitions of the experiment.

Scientific inquiry

Scientific inquiry is the impetus and catalyst for all scientific research and experimentation. It grows from questions about the observed world and gives us a template with which to apply the scientific method. Steps in scientific inquiry include the following principles:

1. Determination and scope of the questions to be investigated are the first step. These may range from simple to extremely complex questions to be explored by scientists.

2. The design, strategy, and method of the inquiry are then carefully considered, and a model for the inquiry is constructed.

3. The formulation of theories and models based on the careful observation of objective, unbiased data then follows. This formulation is derived from the scope of the scientific inquiry and the questions to be investigated.

4. Analysis of possible alternative conclusions drawn from the models and results of experimentation follows.

5. Postulating a theory or constructing a scientific statement based on conclusions is the next logical step.

6. Defending the scientific statement against alternative hypotheses is a critical function of scientific inquiry.

7. Defense of the theory or conclusion against critical analysis is the final step in the process.

Hypothetico-deductive process

The *hypothetico-deductive process* states that to have an idea and then formulate a hypothesis are essentially creative processes, driven by eons of human experience. Statements about reality are the logical conclusions of observed experience. Such creative propositions are the basis for scientific inquiry. Empirical evidence must then validate these hypotheses. Creative inspiration and scientific validation are interdependent aspects of scientific inquiry. New observations often are the catalyst for creative new theories. Science thus proceeds through creative thinking and scientific validation. There are criticisms of the hypothetico-deductive process: The problem of deduction points out that the original hypothesis may be proved wrong in the future, thus invalidating all subsequent conclusions. The problem of induction, building a theory from generalizations, is that any generalization may be proved wrong by future objective observations. This hypothetico-deductive process, and its problems, is a fascinating subject to philosophers of science.

Importance of a hypothesis

It is important to form a hypothesis in order to make a tentative explanation that accounts for an unbiased observation. To be scientific, the hypothesis must be testable through experimentation. Careful construction of the experiment provides that predictions derived from the hypothesis are valid. The hypothesis must be formulated in a manner designed to

provide a framework for evaluating the results of an experiment. In many scientific experiments, a hypothesis is posited in negative terms because scientists may accept logically plausible ideas until they are proven false. It is more difficult to prove that a hypothesis is true because its validity must be proven in all possible situations under endless variable conditions. Scientists tend to construct hypotheses for testing by creating experiments that might prove them false. If they succeed, the hypothesis must be modified or discarded.

Variables in hypothesis testing

Testing a hypothesis is the key to both scientific inquiry and the scientific method. While testing, all variables of the experiment must be strictly controlled except the one being studied. Variables, by their definition, are the processes subject to change. Examples of this in a typical experiment would be the degree of heat or light. In an experiment there are three types of variables:

- The variable to be tested. Known as the independent variable.
- Dependent variables. These are dynamic conditions that may change because of the independent variable.
- Controlled variables. These are conditions that are held constant so they do not affect the independent variable.

A well-constructed experiment changes one independent variable at a time, observing the effects it may have on

- 106 -

dependent variables. Only one independent variable at a time may be manipulated, so the experiment will yield a clear cause and effect result. If more than one independent variable were applied, the experimenter could not be sure which variable caused the result. This would invalidate the conclusions of the experiment.

Criticisms of the deductive model

The deductive model of the scientific method has the following criticisms:

- The deductive model fails to make logical distinctions among explanations, predictions, and descriptions of things to be explained.
- The deductive model is restrictive: It excludes most scientific examples.
- The deductive model is too inclusive: It admits data that cannot be explained.
- The deductive model requires an account of cause, law, and probability, which are basically unsound.
- The deductive model leaves out the elements of context, judgment, and understanding.

Prediction

These are the two widely accepted definitions of scientific prediction:
In the language of science, *prediction* is stating in advance the outcome from testing a theory or hypothesis in a controlled experiment. Based on objective observation of data, scientists move from observation of facts to a general explanation, or hypothesis, which must be confirmed by testing through experimentation.

Another definition of prediction favored by scientific philosophers is the ability of a hypothesis to lead to deductions of scientific statements that could not be anticipated when the hypothesis was posited. In this sense, prediction means what the scientist can verify from what he or she has deduced from the hypothesis.

Measuring, organizing, and classifying data

Measuring data is a crucial part of the scientific process. Measurements are most useful if they are quantified— expressed in numbers. Measuring is the process of determining variables such as time, space, and temperature of objects and processes in precise numbers. The metric system is the universal standard of measurement in science.

Data must be organized in a practical, useful manner to be valuable. Scientists use graphs, charts, tables, and other organizational tools to make data more useful.

Data must then be classified—grouped into organizational schemes for easy access and use. These schemes attempt to organize the maximum amount of useful data in a format that scientists can use.

Although these steps may be less glamorous than other areas of science, they are essential.

Verification and confirmation of data

A critical distinction should be made between confirmation and verification of scientific data. *Verification* establishes once and for all the truth of the statement. *Confirmation* is the testing of claims to see how true they are. For a claim to be testable, an experiment must be devised to ensure the validity of the results. A claim can only be confirmed when we know the conditions for verification. A claim confirmation is always relative to the testing procedures. Test results must always be objective and observable. Actually, no factual claim can ever be verified because there is always the possibility of new evidence appearing that proves the claim false. A scientific law must also be confirmed by making predictions based on unbiased, observable data.

Laboratory safety

The following basic rules should be supplemented by standards appropriate to individual laboratories:

- Hazardous areas must be identified and warnings posted regarding risks.
- A hazard containment plan must be in effect and readily available.
- Safe control of airflow must be maintained at all times.
- Safe work practices must be taught to all who work in the lab.

- Proper maintenance of laboratory equipment must be enforced.
- Safe storage of hazardous material must be implemented.
- Procedures for safe disposal of hazardous wastes must be followed at all times.
- An updated emergency procedure manual must be available.
- A complete emergency first aid kit should be accessible at all times.
- Regular education on the basics of lab safety should be implemented.

Scientific theories

Some major scientific theories include:
- The once widely accepted *received view theory* is based on an analysis of theories empirically devised from deductive axiomatic systems. This theory has been widely criticized.
- The *model theory* states that a model may be constructed to correlate to a real system of relationships, and it can be used to simulate real systems. This allows the model to be manipulated and controlled and be able to predict the dynamics of the real system.
- *Mechanistic theories* do not attempt to fit phenomena into a set of inferential patterns but focus on the mechanism by which data is produced or realized.
- Scientific theories have many different structures that may be

applied in various realms of science.

Objectivity of science

The standard view of science is that it is objective above all. Science has a methodology that ensures against bias and prejudices and is testable by any qualified observer. The most obvious criticism of this tenet is that nothing can be viewed objectively because of the nature of the senses and their ability to distort observations. Other criticisms have arisen, led by Paul Feyerabend, Herbert Marcuse, and Nicholas Maxwell. Each has posited a different paradigm, in which science is viewed as one tradition among many. These radical thinkers (among many others) have challenged the objectivity of science on philosophical grounds. However, their arguments, while raising good questions, supply few rewarding answers. The most valid challenge to the objectivity of science is the difficulty of knowing if any observation is valid because of the inherent subjectivity of the observer. Quantum mechanics has provided new fuel for the question of an individual's ability to observe objectively.

Scientific laws

Scientific principles must meet a high standard to be classified as laws:

- Scientific laws must be true, not just probable. A highly probable principle may still be proven false.
- Laws are statements of patterns found in nature.

- Laws may have a universal form but be stated conditionally. For example, the statement "All living human beings breathe," may be restated "If a thing is a living human being it must breathe."
- Laws refer to a general, not a particular, class.
- Laws have purely qualitative predicates.
- Laws must have a formal language of expression to be fully understood. Such a language does not exist now.
- Laws may be probabilistic. For example, a law may state "Eight percent of all dogs are terriers."

Motivation for doing science

The motivation for doing science has fascinated society since the beginnings of scientific inquiry. Motives internal to the process of scientific research include scientific curiosity and the pleasure of doing pure research. Motives generated by the scientific community are the desire for a scientific reputation and corresponding influence in a scientific field. External influences on scientific research are the attractions of public fame, the desire to provide useful applications for society, the need for funding, and the ambition of influencing public and private policy. The desire to profit financially is an additional incentive. Although most scientists do earn a living from their work, there is a clear sense that scientific curiosity is the primary motive. No activity can count as scientific unless it answers the desire to know and understand the truth about some aspect of the physical or psychological world. Thus, multiple motives inspire scientists, and the common factor for all is scientific inquiry.

Neutrality of science

Science may be regarded as value neutral by society. This scientific neutrality is supported by the following arguments:
1. Science provides us with knowledge of how the world works and the consequences of our interventions in it, but it does not indicate whether or when such interventions should be made. Science is like a map that can tell us how to get to many places but does not tell us where to go.
2. Although scientists may welcome applications of their work, the primary focus is on the advancement of knowledge for its own sake.
3. The applications of scientific knowledge are for society to decide. The scientist is the servant of the people, using his or her expertise to attain goals others have set.
All three of these arguments are open to challenge and debate, and many exceptions can be found for each.

Limitations of science

There are clear limits on what science can explain. The demand for objectivity both strengthens knowledge we gain from scientific experiments and limits what we can explore. Beyond the realm of scientific inquiry are such questions as "Why does anything exist?" or "What is the meaning of life?" These are subjective questions that do not lend themselves easily to scientific inquiry. These questions, and others like them, come from within, and their conclusions, not validated by science, shape the very fabric of a society. They attempt to give meaning to what may be viewed as chaos. Periodically, science will impact these subjective conclusions with new evidence. For example, the theory of evolution is regarded as blasphemy by many religious fundamentalists. These conflicts may cause great upheavals in society, leaving many to wonder how science and religious belief can be reconciled. Ultimately, observation of the external world must stand as the true test of science.

Arguments against science

The reasons usually given to do science include intellectual curiosity, theoretical interest, and the potential usefulness to society. But what are the arguments about not doing science? They may be summarized as follows:

- Any scientific inquiry uses someone's time and effort. The opportunity cost of this time and effort must be evaluated: What other activities must be ignored if time and energy are used in scientific endeavors?
- Resource allocation is the other argument against scientific research. When a project demands significant funds, questions can obviously be raised about the relative value of using

the funds on one project rather than another. We are currently engaged in a national debate about allocating huge sums for scientific projects such as space exploration or the Human Genome Project. The billions of dollars needed to fund these projects could be used in a variety of less-costly projects that may benefit society more.

These objections are raised about large national projects, but they may be equally applicable to any proposal for a scientific investigation.

Practical technology and science

A famous example of a practical technological breakthrough with vast industrial applications, which also stimulated the development of theoretical science, is the invention of the steam engine. James Watt, the developer of the steam engine, was an engineer more than a scientist. Watt's contribution was a modification of existing principles that led to a much more efficient steam engine. This had a huge impact on technology, economics, and science. Watt's research led to fundamental research in the theory of heat and the science of thermodynamics, with its general equations of the transfer of energy. Thus, though Watt did not directly contribute to pure science, his work formed the foundation for important pure research. We may speculate, had social and educational conditions been different, that Watt would have pursued a scientific career rather than an engineering career.

Science history provides many more examples of similar cases, indicating that pure and applied science often go hand in hand in advancing human knowledge.

Effects of biotechnical innovations on society

There are many biotechnical innovations that are beneficial to specific individuals in society that may be harmful to society as a whole. An example is the ability of parents to choose the sex of their offspring. This choice offers appealing benefits to individuals who may prefer one sex over another for a variety of reasons. However, if these choices lead to a 80/20 ratio of the sexes, it will be harmful to the population as a whole. An outcome of multiple individual choices would then amount to a net harm to society. Society moves to counter collective action problems by social pressure, legislation, and control. These countermeasures have the potential for altering society in unforeseen ways. The new power of institutions seeking to solve scientific problems that impact society may be the most alarming result of the meeting of science and technology.

Scientists and nuclear weapons

The development of atomic weapons was one of the greatest (or most notorious) scientific feats of the twentieth century. The construction of the first atomic bomb and subsequent development of more-sophisticated weapons remain among the most controversial issues in science. Scientists such as A.O.C. Nier, Leo Szilard,

Niels Bohr, Robert Oppenheimer, Edward Teller, and a score of other brilliant physicists contributed to the Manhattan Project—the crash program to develop an atomic weapon to end World War II. The success of this and subsequent projects had both beneficial and negative effects for the world and for mankind. Many of the scientists involved had grave second thoughts about the use of these weapons. One moral of this fascinating and complex story is that scientists who develop powerful scientific applications can never be sure that the science will be used in ways of which they will approve.

Human Genome Project

The *Human Genome Project* was conceived by scientists in the nuclear weapons lab at Los Alamos National Laboratory, presumably to ensure the future of their jobs and to do more-positive research. The project plans to map out all human genes. Controversy swirls around this project: Many feel it is a misuse of vitally needed research funds. Others have concerns about the possible uses of such knowledge of human genetics. At the heart of these questions is whether we want to develop the science of genetic engineering, and if so, to what extent. Information gleaned from the project could give us the power to tinker with human nature itself. There is a sharp division of opinion on this matter. On the one hand, scientific curiosity, technological pressures, and the drive for adventure make this an appealing project. Yet, on the other hand, critics say the project will raise new and difficult

medical and ethical issues that will create division and acrimony.

Birth of the environmental movement

Rachel Carson is described as the mother of the environmental movement that began in the 1960s. Her book *Silent Spring* awakened public concern about the hazards of pesticides, and it spurred an awareness of environmental problems.

The agricultural chemicals industry branded Carson as a hysterical woman without professional credentials at war with the agricultural economy. They claimed Carson had grossly distorted the actual facts and provided no scientific evidence for her conclusions. Carson's specific arguments were never refuted, although her rhetoric has been called inflammatory. Carson never called for a ban on pesticides, but she was concerned about their indiscriminate use and its effects on ecosystems. Her legacy includes the myriad environmental groups formed after her book and the establishment of the Environment Protection Agency. Her work raised public awareness of the protection of natural habitats, and it remains a milestone in the science of ecology.

Science and ethics

Debates over issues paramount to science and ethics are rarely resolved unambiguously. Ethical conclusions should be based on reason, logic, and accepted principles that represent a consensus of current thinking on a question. Education and debate are important in clarifying issues and allowing intelligent participation in a democratic process. Deciding issues of science and society usually requires an examination of individual cases. Generalizations in these areas tend to lead to extreme positions that exclude mainstream opinions. Both intrinsic and consequential arguments for or against any question may be advanced. There are no blanket solutions to most problems involving science, technology, and societal ethics.

Good and evil effects of science on society

The applications of science have produced countless benefits for society, and the potential exists for many more benefits. However, science has been put to many negative and destructive ends in warfare and weaponry and in the less-obvious examples of pollution and the effects of radiation. The cost-benefit equation will be debated endlessly, with few real general conclusions drawn. We must live with the fact that science is used for both beneficial and destructive purposes by society, and, more alarmingly, it is often difficult to predict which are which. We must welcome the benefits that science provides, while understanding that these benefits may have hidden costs, and that even the best-planned technologies have unforeseen consequences. It must be acknowledged that there will always be forces in society using science for their own ends and not necessarily for the benefit of society.

Science is neither a demon nor panacea; it should be considered on the merits of individual research.

Sexism in science

Two examples from the recent history of science illustrate the ongoing concern of sexism:

- Rosalind Franklin was not given appropriate credit for developing a great deal of important data leading to the discovery of the structure of DNA. James Watson, the father of DNA discovery, has been accused of downplaying the contributions made by Ms. Franklin. This case is complex and appears to involve much more than gender-based discrimination, but there is little doubt sexism played a role.
- A more obvious case of sex discrimination can be made for Jocelyn Bell in the discovery of stars known as pulsars. Bell, a member of a team headed by Antony Hewish at Cambridge University, made initial observations that eventually led to the discovery of pulsars (a type of tiny neutron stars). Hewish received the Nobel Prize for this discovery, but Bell was not included in the honors. Hewish later commented "Jocelyn was a jolly good girl, but she was just doing her job." This statement would be understood as blatant sexism today.

Despite the increased number of prominent female scientists today, there still remains a concern that they do not always share in the credit deserved.

Newton's second law

Newton's second law is applicable only if the force is the net external force. It will not apply in situations in which mass changes, either from gaining or losing material, or because the object travels close to the speed of light where relativistic effects have to be included. It is expressed:

F (net external force) = ma (mass of object x acceleration)

Newton's second law has its limitations because it is not a fundamental principle like the conservation laws. The net force should be defined as the rate change of momentum. Because mass changes as the speed approaches the speed of light, F = ma is viewed only as a non-relative relationship applied to the acceleration of constant mass objects. It is extremely important in predicting motion under these constraints despite these limitations.

Galilean equivalence principle

The Galilean equivalence principle is the equivalence of inertial and gravitational masses. It is also called the "weak equivalence principle." Most important among the principle's consequences is as it applies to objects that freely fall. Take for example, an object with inertial and gravitational masses m and M. This says the ratio of gravitational mass of any object is equal to some constant, K, if and only if all objects fall at the same rate in a particular gravitational field. This is called the "universality of freefall."

Noether's theorem

Noether's theorem expresses a one-to-one correspondence between conservation laws and symmetries. The equivalence is prevalent in all physical laws based on the action of principle defined over symplectic space, a mathematical vector space. Symmetry is defined in this since, the covariance of the form a physical law takes in the case of a one-dimensional Lie group, a mathematical manifold, of transformations satisfying certain technical prerequisites. The theorem's principles include:

- Energy is conserved if physical laws do not vary under time translations.
- Momentum is conserved if physical laws do not vary under spatial translations.
- Angular momentum is conserved if physical laws do not vary under rotations.

A Noether charge is a physical amount conserved as a result of a continuous symmetry of an underlying system.

Law of Conservation of Mass

The Law of Conservation of Mass in a chemical reaction is commonly stated as follows:

In a chemical reaction, matter is neither created nor destroyed.

What this means is that there will always be the same total mass of material after a reaction as before. This allows for predicting how molecules will combine by balanced equations in which the number of each type of atom is the same on either side of the equation. For example, two hydrogen molecules combine with one oxygen molecule to form water. This is a balanced chemical equation because the number of each type of atom is same on both sides of the arrow. It has to balance because the reaction obeys the Law of Conservation of Mass.

Law of Conservation of Energy

The Law of Conservation of Energy is simply a restatement of the First Law of Thermodynamics. It maintains that the total energy that flows into a system has to be equal the total energy that flows out of the system, plus any change in the energy contained within the system. A more common formulation is that energy can be neither created nor destroyed, it can only be converted from one form to another.

Law of Definite Proportion or Constant Composition

The Law of Definite Proportion or Constant Composition is usually attributed to Dalton and/or Proust and says "Regardless of the method of separation, a pure compound will always contain the same elements in the same proportion by mass." Dalton specifically contributed to the law by the inclusion of the atomic hypothesis. He reasoned that because these elements were atoms that were indivisible, each of the pure compounds "should contain the same proportion of these atoms regardless of the method of preparation."

Einstein's Theory of Relativity

Relativity is comprised of special relativity and general relativity. Special relativity relates that those observers in inertial reference frames, in uniform motion relative to each other, cannot perform experiments to find out which is stationary. This is the principle of relativity, which says basically that regardless of an observer's velocity or position in the universe, all physical laws will appear constant. It was in this context that Einstein found that the speed of light in a vacuum had to be the same for all the observers despite their motion or the motion of the light source. General relativity is a geometrical theory which reasons that the presence of mass and energy will curve spacetime, which is a model that combines to form the space-time continuum, and that the curvature will affect the path of free particles. This includes the path of light. It uses differential geometry and the generalized quantity of tensors to describe gravitation without using the force of gravity. The theory postulates that all observers should be equivalent, not only those that move with uniform speed.

Newton's law of inertia

Newton's First Law of Motion describes inertia: "Every body perseveres in its state of being at rest or of moving uniformly straight ahead except insofar as it is compelled to change its state by forces impressed." This concept is still the classical physics standard but has been expanded and refined over time. This is especially true given developments in understanding relativity and quantum mechanics. Copernicus theorized in the 16th century that the earth and those things on it were in constant motion around the sun and therefore never at rest. Galileo built on that model, recognizing the nature of motion and thus came up with the first modern definition of inertia: "A body moving on a level surface will continue in the same direction at a constant speed unless disturbed."

Newton's Third Law

Newton's Third Law states: All forces in the universe happen in equal but oppositely directed pairs. No isolated forces exist. For each force that is external acting on an object, a force of equal magnitude but oppositely directed acts back on that object that was using the external force. A force of one part of a system, as related to external forces, will be countered by a reactive force on a different part of the system. Thus, an isolated system cannot exert a net force on a system as a whole. Newton's Third Law states that if the forces of an unspecified nature on two masses arise from those pair of masses, they must be equal in magnitude but opposite in direction in order that no net force will arise from forces that are purely internal.

Conservation of momentum

Momentum seems to constantly appear conserved. Without outside forces, a system will have an omnipresent total momentum or a property implied by Newton's law of inertia, which was his first law of motion. Newton's law of reciprocal actions states that forces acting in between systems are equal, which is equal to the conservation of momentum. Momentum also has special properties in which inside a closed system it always is conserved although it is not conserved in inelastic collisions. Elastic collisions, such as two pool balls hitting each other, conserve kinetic energy. Inelastic collisions do not conserve kinetic energy. An example of this is when two objects strike each other and stick together after the collision.

Oppenheimer-Phillips process

The Oppenheimer-Phillips process is a form of nuclear reaction that is also known as strip reaction. In the reaction, a nucleus will react with the neutron of a deuterium core but the proton would not have the energy to overcome the Coulomb barrier. For example:

$$12C(d,p)13C$$

J. Robert Oppenheimer and Melba Phillips described this process in 1935. Oppenheimer went on to be known for his role of scientific head for the

Manhattan Project during World War II (which developed the first nuclear weapons at Los Alamos laboratory in New Mexico). Phillips studied under Oppenheimer and was also known for her refusal to testify before a U.S. Senate Judiciary subcommittee on internal security. It led to her dismissal from Brooklyn College.

Important terms

Quarks - Quarks are, in particle physics, subatomic particles. They are thought to be both indivisible and elemental. Objects composed of quarks are known as hadrons. Well known hadron examples include protons and neutrons.

Hadrons - Hadrons are subatomic particles which experience the strong nuclear force. These are not fundamental particles but rather are made up of fermions called quarks and antiquarks and of bosons called gluons. Gluons are what mediate the color force binding the quarks together.

Leptons - Leptons are one of the two groups of matter particles. There are three pairs of leptons, each pair consisting of an electrically charged particle and a neutrino. The best-known pair is the electron and the electron neutrino. The others are the muon with the muon neutrino and the tau with the tau neutrino. Leptons are subject to the electromagnetic and weak interactions.

Fermions - Fermions are particles forming anti-symmetrical composite quantum states. The spin-statistics theorem says that fermions have a half-integer spin. If one may visualize a particle with a ½ spin, then one might imagine fermions being rotated by two full rotations in order to return to their initial state.

Specific heat - Specific heat is the amount of heat per unit mass needed to raise the temperature by one degree Celsius.

Heat of fusion - Heat of fusion is the energy that is needed to change a gram of a substance from a solid state to a liquid state without changing its temperature.

Heat of vaporization - Heat of vaporization is the energy needed to change a gram of liquid into a gas at its boiling point.

Calorie - A calorie is a measurement of energy. It has been replaced in most areas with the joule, but is still commonly used for measuring the amount of energy that is obtained from food.

British Thermal Unit - The British Thermal Unit or Btu is a unit of energy used in the United States and has been replaced by the joule in many areas. A Btu is the amount of heat needed to raise the temperature of one pound avoirdupois of water by one degree Fahrenheit. It takes 143 Btu to melt a pound of ice. A Btu often is used to describe a fuel's heat value and Btu per hour is used for measuring heating and cooling power for various systems. One Btu is equal to about 252 calories or about 1060 joules.

Anion - A negatively charged ion produced when an atom gains an electron. The nonmetallic atoms in compounds tend to form anions because they exert a stronger pull on neighboring electrons.

Cation - A positively charged ion produced when an atom loses an electron.

Metals tend to hold their electrons relatively loosely, so they are lost more easily.

Binary compound - A compound containing two elements bound by either ionic or covalent bonds.

Ternary compound - A compound containing three elements bound by ionic or covalent bonds.

Metals - elements that gain electrons in chemical reactions. When their neighboring atoms lose electrons to the metals, those atoms form cations.

Non-metals: elements that lose electrons in chemical reactions. When their neighboring atoms gain the lost electrons, they form anions.

Ions - Ions are particles containing a positive or negative charge; they may be either single atoms or polyatomic ions. Ions form ionic bonds through the attraction of opposite electromagnetic charges.

Outer energy level - The outer energy level is the highest numbered level of an atom containing electrons. Energy levels of atoms are sometimes called shells, or energy shells, and only the electrons in this outer level are available to form chemical bonds.

Valence electrons - Valence electrons are those electrons inhabiting the outer energy level. They are available to form bonds through sharing (covalent bonds) or electrostatic attraction (ionic bonds).

Octet rule - The octet rule describes the tendency of atoms to share, lose, or gain electrons until their outer energy level contains a total of eight. When eight is reached, the atom is in its most stable

form and is less likely to bond with others.

Polar bond - A polar bond is a covalent bond between two atoms of unequal electronegativity. One atom attracts the molecule's electrons more strongly, creating regions of uneven electrical charge within the molecule.

Polar molecule - A polar molecule is a molecule in which a polar bond creates an uneven charge.

Bond moment - The bond moment measures the polarity of a polar bond in a molecule.

Dipole moment - A dipole moment is a measurement of two opposing polarities within a structure and the distance separating them.

Delocalization - Delocalization is the tendency of electrons to be only loosely bound to the nuclei of their parent atoms. They then become bonding electrons in a number of neighboring atoms. Benzene (C_6H_6), for instance, shares electrons from the C atoms amongst all the other C in the compound. Delocalization accounts for the high electrical conductivity of metals.

Single, double, and triple bonds - Single, double, and triple bonds form when atoms share one, two, and three pairs of electrons, respectively.

Metals - Metals are elements that are good conductors of heat and electricity; tend to form positive ions, have positive oxidation numbers, have generally high melting points, ductility, and malleability.

Nonmetals - Nonmetals are usually very poor conductors of heat and electricity and can have more varied properties than a metal, and they form negative ions, have negative oxidation numbers, and form brittle solids.

Metalloids - Metalloids have properties that fall between metals and nonmetals.
Anion - An anion is a negatively charged ion. It is formed by adding electrons to atoms or molecules.

Cation - A cation is a positively charged ion that is formed by removal of electrons from atoms or molecules.

Ionic crystal - An ionic crystal is a crystal that is made up of two or more elements. The positive and negative ions are arranged in a definitive pattern. They are held together by electrostatic attraction. Some examples include sodium chloride and cesium chloride.

Lattice - A lattice is a three-dimensional arrangement of points. It is used to describe positions of particles such as atoms, ions or molecules in a crystalline solid. The lattice structure may be examined by using X-ray diffraction techniques.

Mixture - A mixture is made of two or more substances that are combined in various proportions with each retaining its own specific properties. A mixture's components may be separated by physical means, that is without making and breaking chemical bonds. An example would be table salt being completely dissolved in water.

Heterogeneous mixture - Heterogeneous mixtures are those in which the composition and properties are not uniform throughout the entire sample. Examples include concrete and wood.

Homogeneous mixture - Homogeneous mixtures are those in which the composition and properties are uniform throughout the entire sample.

Pure substance - Pure substances are those substances with composition that is constant. They may fit the classification as either a compound or an element.

Cyclic compound - Cyclic compounds are hydrocarbons whose bonding structure creates ring-shaped molecules. Hydrocarbons also occur in the form of long chains.

Amino acid - Amino acids are the building blocks of peptides and proteins. They are carboxylic acids with an amino group ($-NH_2$) bonded to the carboxyl group. Common amino acids include glycine, cystine, tryptophan, and phenylalanine.

Carbon tetravalency - Carbon tetravalency refers to the tendency of carbon atoms to form four covalent bonds with other atoms in organic compounds. This predictability is important because all organic compounds contain carbon. Its tetravalency, due to its four valence electrons, enables inferences and predictions about properties and reactions of organic compounds.

Benzene - Benzene, C_6H_6, is an important cyclic compound in organic chemistry which forms the backbone of many other compounds when H bound to the ring's C is replaced by other groups or elements.

Aromatic compounds - Aromatic compounds are compounds with benzene as a base. Many of them have a strong odor.

Carbohydrates - Carbohydrates (also called sugars, starch, and cellulose) are complex organic molecules used as sources of energy by many life forms.

They contain only C, H, and O, and occur in many sizes from simple forms, called monosaccharides, to complex polysaccharides.

Lipids - Lipids are also called fats in their solid state and oils in their liquid state. They can be broken down through catalyzed reactions and separated from their constituent fatty acids. They are insoluble in water and are vital parts of living cells.

Proteins - Proteins are complex molecules formed of long chains of peptides (polypeptides) and are fundamental to many living functions, including cell construction. Collagens, elastins, keratins, and antibodies are common proteins.

Peptides - Peptides are compounds of two or more linked amino acids.

Enzymes - Enzymes are specialized compounds acting as catalysts for reactions necessary for life.

Aldol condensation - Aldol condensation is a reaction in which two aldehyde molecules join to form a product called an aldol, containing both aldehyde and alcohol functional groups. It is an important reaction in several industrial processes such as the production of insect repellent.

Diels-Alder reaction - The Diels-Alder reaction is a cycloaddition reaction in which two unsaturated hydrocarbons combine to form a ring. It involves a conjugated diene (an unsaturated hydrocarbon with two C=C double bonds) and either an alkene or alkyne. The two terminal atoms of the diene bond to the C atoms of the alkene double bond to form a ring with five C—C bonds and one C=C bond; the double bond of the former diene remains while the double bonds of the alkene are "lost." These reactions are stereospecific: they occur only with specific isomeric configurations.

Metabolism – Metabolism is the cell's ability to extract energy from its environment and use that energy for cellular activities.

Photosynthesis – Photosynthesis is the process of cells converting sunlight energy into chemical energy.

Theory – A theory is a set of hypotheses that explains an aspect of the natural world.

Catenation - Catenation is the ability of elements to form long chains of identical atoms. Carbon is the most remarkable element in this regard, forming long chains or rings which were the first compounds to be identified and named according to the rules of organic nomenclature.

Hydrocarbons - Hydrocarbons are molecules composed solely of H and C atoms and are the basis of organic chemistry. The C atoms form the "backbone" of the molecule to which the H atoms attach.

Alkanes - Hydrocarbons arranged in rings or chains without functional groups often form the roots of organic nomenclature. This class of compounds is called alkanes. The suffix –ane identifies these compounds as alkanes, while a Greek prefix shows the number of C atoms. Some examples include pentane (5C), octane (8C), decane (10C). Some more familiar alkanes (methane, propane, butane, ethane) were named prior to the development of standardized nomenclature, so do not conform to these standards.

Cycloalkanes - When the C chains form rings, they are called cycloalkanes.
Superimposable - A superimposable molecule is one that can be placed over another molecule and occupy the same three dimensional space.

Mirror-image - A molecule can be imagined as having a mirror-image—a reflection of itself. Not all mirror images are identical. For instance the reflection of a left-handed desk is right handed and nonsuperimposable. If the mirror image of an object is identical, it is said to be superimposable.

Chiral - Molecules that are not superimposable on their mirror images are chiral.

Stereogenic center - A stereogenic center is a central atom of a molecule which has other atoms or molecules bonded to it in such a way that the overall molecule is chiral.

Enantiomers - Enantiomers are nonsuperimposable isomers.

Unsaturated hydrocarbon - Unsaturated hydrocarbons are organic molecules in rings or chains in which C atoms are joined with double or triple bonds; therefore not every C is bonded to an H atom. A saturated hydrocarbon has the maximum possible number of H atoms because they are joined with C atoms by single bonds.

Alkene - Alkenes are hydrocarbon chains characterized by C=C double bonds. In naming organic compounds, the longest carbon chain or ring chain forms the root; the –ene suffix indicates an alkene, and a Greek prefix indicates the number of

alkenes present. Example: trimethyl hexane contains three methyl molecules and five (from hexa) alkenes.

Cycloalkene - When alkenes form rings, they are called cycloalkenes.

Alkyne - Alkynes are hydrocarbon chains characterized by C⌐C triple bonds. In nomenclature, the –yne suffix indicates an alkyne, and a Greek prefix indicates the number of alkynes present. Therefore, a compound called dibutyl decyne contains two butyl molecules and ten (from deca-) alkynes.

Cycloalkyne - When alkynes form rings, they are called cycloalkenes.

Ligand – A ligand is an atom or group of atoms which bonds to a central atom in reactions, assuming a central atom can be determined (they sometimes cannot).

Bridging ligand - If a ligand connects two or more atoms or parts of the structure, it is called a bridging ligand; these usually serve to bridge between two metallic atoms due to the ionic bonding propensities of metals.

Chelation - Chelation refers to the formation of bonds or intramolecular attractions on specific binding sites within ligands.

Leaving group - An atom or group that detaches from another atom or group in a given reaction is called the leaving group.

Entering group - An entering group is an atom or group which forms bonds with an existing atom or group of any given reaction. Groups can enter or leave on both sides of the reaction equation.

Atomic number - All atoms can be identified by the number of protons and neutrons that they contain. The atomic number (often denoted as Z) is the

- 121 -

number of protons in the nucleus of each atom of an element. In a neutral atom the number of protons is equal to the number of electrons.

Atomic mass number - The atomic mass number (often denoted as A) is the total number of neutrons and protons present in the nucleus of an atom of an element. In general the mass number is given by: mass number = number of protons + number of neutrons = atomic number + number of neutrons

Atoms of a given element typically do not all have the same mass. Three types of hydrogen atoms exist, for example, which differ only in their number of neutrons. They are hydrogen, which has one proton and no neutrons; deuterium which has one proton and one neutron; and tritium which has one proton and two neutrons. Isotopes - Atoms that have the same atomic number but different mass numbers are called isotopes.

Interfacial defects - An atom's environment at the surface is different from that of an atom in bulk because the number of neighbors, or coordination, decreases. This brings in unbalanced forces resulting in relaxation or reconstruction. The former is when the lattice spacing decreases. The latter is the crystal structure changes. Density of atoms in regions including grain boundaries is smaller than the bulk value because space happens in the interface. Interfaces and surfaces are very reactive. It is unusual that impurities segregate there. Grains tend to grow in size at the expense of small grains in order to minimize energy due to energy being required to form a surface. This happens by diffusion that accelerates at elevated temperatures.

Volume defects - A normal volume defect is porosity. It often takes place during processing in the solid. Snow, a highly porous ice, is a common example.

Stellar nucleosynthesis - Stellar nucleosynthesis is the term used for nuclear reactions that happen in stars to make the nuclei of heavier elements. The process can be understood by realizing that the energy that comes from nuclear reactions account for the Sun's longevity as a source of heat and light. Its prime energy source is the fusion of hydrogen and helium, which takes place at a minimum temperature of 3 million kelvins.

Supernova nucleosynthesis - Supernova nucleosynthesis relates to nuclear fusion or nuclear fission of matter inside supernovas. A neutron capture process for radioactive elements, the R-process, happens during supernova nucleosynthesis. This process takes place in high neutron densities with high temperatures.

Geiger counters - Geiger counters were among the initial detection devices for ionized gas. The Geiger-Müller counter is a sealed cylinder with a polymer window which contains gas and a wire. High voltage is applied between the cathode, which is the cylinder, and the wire, an anode. As X-ray photons enter the cylinder the gas is ionized and becomes more conducting which creates a current flow. The peak of this current is known as a count.

Scintillators - Scintillators are detectors in which some materials can convert an X photon to a visible photon. Their main advantage is that adequate images can be obtained while the patient is given a much lower dose of X-rays.

Dissolve - To dissolve is to reduce a compound to smaller and smaller sizes until it is distributed evenly and interacts on a molecular level with the solvent in a solution.

Solute - Solute is the target substance or substances dissolved in a solution; a teaspoon of sugar may be the solute in a cup of tea.

Solvent - Solvent is the medium in which the solute is dissolved, such as the water in saltwater.

Solution - A solution is the mixture of a solvent and its solute(s). Solutions are homogeneous and symmetrical because any portion of a solution has the same composition and contents of any other portion. Components of solutions can be separated from each other but not through simple means like filtration. When the concentration of a solute is constant, the solution is saturated. Unsaturated solution simply has less solute.

Solubility - Solubility is the amount of a substance that dissolves in a solvent.

Activity - In terms of solutions, activity is an alternative concentration used in calculations instead of actual concentrations. Using the alternative allows equations designed for use with ideal solutions to be used with real solutions.

Aeration - Aeration is a process for preparing saturated solutions by bubbling air (i.e. gases) through it. Aqueous solutions may also be sprayed into a

closed container of gases as another method of aeration.

Colloid - A colloid is a mixture (not always a solution) containing tiny particles suspended in a host material. The particles, which may be solids, liquids, or gases, do not drop out of the mixture, but pass through most filters, are larger than molecules and do not interact on a molecular level.

Aerosol - Aerosols are colloids containing particles of solids or liquids suspended in a gaseous host. Smoke is an aerosol; its solid particles of unconsumed matter are suspended in hot gases produced by the fuel that is consumed.

Eutectic mixture - Eutectic mixtures are those of two or more substances whose concentrations produce a lower melting point than mixtures of the same substances with different concentrations.

Emulsion - An emulsion is a colloid containing liquid particles suspended in another liquid. Although the particles and the host are liquids, they do not mix on a molecular level, so are not considered solutions.

Foam - is a colloid containing bubbles of gas suspended in a solid or liquid host. Whipped cream is a liquid foam; Styrofoam is a solid foam.

Azeotrope - An azeotrope is a type of solution which retains its original composition when distilled. For example, when some alcohols are boiled, the vapor shows the same concentration as the liquid solution.

Dilution - Dilution is the process of lowering the concentration of a solution by adding additional solvent.

Ebulliometry - Ebulliometry is the process of calculating the molecular weight of a solute by observing the boiling point elevation of the solution.

Osmometry - Osmometry is a series of calculations used to determine the average molecular weight of a solvent in solution based on the solution's osmotic pressure.

Hypertonic - Hypertonic refers to a solution with a higher osmotic pressure than surrounding solutions, such as within cells. For example, seawater is hypertonic; when a freshwater fish is placed in seawater, the seawater "draws" water from the fish's cells due to its higher osmotic pressure. The natural "freshwater" balance of the fluids in the fish is disrupted and it dies.

Hypotonic - Hypotonic is simply the reverse: it describes solutions whose osmotic pressure is lower than that of surrounding solutions. For example, distilled water, which has been processed to remove most mineral solutes, is hypotonic; it causes cells to take in water. If volume and concentration are sufficient, cells will even swell and burst in the presence of hypotonic solutions.

Hydronium ions - Hydronium ions are the ionic form (H_3O^+) of water molecules formed when additional H is available in the vicinity of H_2O. They are unstable and exist for only a brief amount of time before reacting in equilibrium to return to the unionized form of the molecule.

Conjugate acid - Conjugate acids and bases are best understood as conjugate pairs. These are acid-base pairs that react to form one another by losing and gaining protons per the Brønsted-Lowry theory.

Conjugate base - A conjugate base is the base form of an acid that has become a base by accepting a proton; the conjugate acid is the substance formed when that base then gives up a proton. Strong acids form weak conjugate bases, while weak acids form strong bases.

Amphoterism - Amphoterism describes a substance having properties of both acids and bases.

Practice Test

Practice Questions

1. Which of the listed chemical species would be expected to have the highest electron affinity?
   a. Na
   b. F
   c. He+
   d. H+
   e. Cl-

2. An analytical standard has a mass of 10.00 g. A student takes five mass measurements and obtains the following results: 9.01 g, 9.05 g, 9.10 g, 8.99 g, and 9.00 g. Which of the following best characterizes the set of measurements?
   a. High accuracy, low precision
   b. High accuracy, high precision
   c. Low accuracy, low precision
   d. Low accuracy, high precision
   e. Flawed due to experimental error

3. Two molecules are enantiomers of each other. They would be expected to have the identical:
   a. Melting point
   b. Boiling point
   c. Magnitude of optical rotation
   d. Heat of combustion
   e. All of the above

4. What is the molecular geometry of SF_6?
   a. Octahedral
   b. Square planar
   c. Tetrahedral
   d. Trigonal bipyramidal
   e. Hexagonal planar

5. Which of the following groups are meta directors when attached to a benzene ring?
   a. Cl
   b. CH3
   c. NO2
   d. NH2
   e. OCH3

6. For most materials, an increase in pressure will
    a. Decrease the boiling point and increase the melting point
    b. Decrease the boiling point and decrease the melting point
    c. Increase the boiling point and increase the melting point
    d. Increase the boiling point and decrease the melting point
    e. Have little effect on either

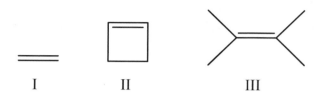

I   II   III

7. Place the alkenes shown above in the correct order of decreasing reactivity towards electrophilic addition reactions.
    a. I>II>III
    b. II>I>III
    c. I>III>II
    d. II>III>I
    e. III>I>II

8. Which of the following transformations leads to an increase in system entropy?
    A.   Water vapor condensing to a liquid
    B.   Ice melting to liquid water
    C. The complete burning of butane in O_2 to produce CO_2 and H_2O
    D. The dissolution of sugar in water
    E.   The separation of a racemic mixture into pure enantiomers

    a. I, III, V
    b. II, III, IV
    c. I, IV, V
    d. II, IV, V
    e. II, III, V

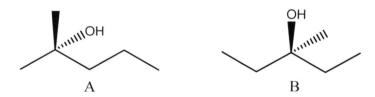

A   B

9. Structures A and B are what relative to each other?
    a. Enantiomers
    b. Diasteriomers
    c. Meso structures
    d. Structural isomers
    e. Stereoisomers

10. The Ksp of AgCl is 1.77×10^{-10}. What is the concentration of Ag^+ ions in a saturated aqueous solution of AgCl?

    a. 1.77×10^{-10} M

    b. 1.33×10^{-5} M

    c. 3.13×10^{-20} M

    d. 8.85×10^{-11} M

    e. 3.54×10^{-10} M

11. The pH of a solution of HCl in water is 4. What is the concentration of HCl in the solution?

    a. 0.1 M

    b. 1.0 M

    c. 0.004 M

    d. 0.0001 M

    e. 0.04 M

12. 5.0 L of an ideal gas at 100 K is heated to 150 k at constant pressure. What will be the new volume of the gas?

    a. 7.5 L

    b. 5.0 L

    c. 3.3 L

    d. 3000.0 L

    e. 10 L

I   II

13. Which of the following reagents would be best at converting I to II?

    a. Br2

    b. HNO3

    c. CrO3

    d. NaBH4

    e. NaOH

14. Which of the following has the halogen acids placed in the correct order of increasing acidity?

    a. HF<HI<HBr<HCl

    b. HF<HCl<HBr<HI

    c. HI<HBr<HCl<HF

    d. HI<HF<HBr<HCl

    e. HBr<HCl<HI<HF

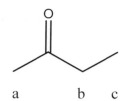

a   b   c

15. What will be the splitting patterns of protons a, b and c in the ^{1}H NMR spectrum of the molecule shown above?

    a. Singlet, triplet, quartet
    b. Singlet doublet, triplet
    c. Triplet, doublet quartet
    d. Singlet, quartet, triplet
    e. Triplet, singlet, quartet

I   II   III   IV   V

16. Which of the structures shown above is not aromatic?

    a. I
    b. II
    c. III
    d. IV
    e. V

17. Which of the following compounds will react the most exothermically with methanol?

    a. NaOH
    b. Acetyl chloride
    c. Phenyl bromide
    d. water
    e. sodium chloride

18. Which analytical method would be least effective at distinguishing between ethyl bromide and ethyl cyanide?

    a. 1H NMR
    b. IR
    c. UV
    d. Mass spec
    e. 13 C NMR

19. A compound contains 85.7 wt% C and 14.3 wt % H. Which of the following is the correct molecular formula?
    a. C2H6
    b. C2H2
    c. C3H6
    d. C4H10
    e. C3H8

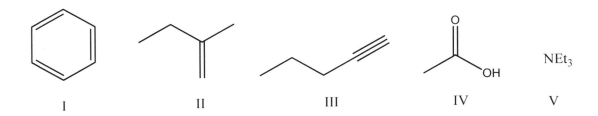

I   II   III   IV   V

20. Which of the compounds shown above is a likely product of the Wittig reaction?
    a. I
    b. II
    c. III
    d. IV
    e. V

21. Diamond and graphite differ primarily in what way?
    a. Molecular weight
    b. Optical activity
    c. Solid phase
    d. Elemental analysis
    e. Radioactivity

22. What is the normality of a 0.25 M solution of H_2SO_4 in water?
    a. 0.25 N
    b. 0.50 N
    c. 0.75 N
    d. 1.5 N

23. What is the correct IUPAC name for the following compound?

a. Chloromethyl butanoate
b. Methyl-chloro butanoate
c. Methyl-chloro butanoic acid
d. Methyl-4-chloro-butanoate
e. 1-chloro-4-methyl butanoate

24. DNA is a biopolymer composed of what primary monomer?
a. Amino acids
b. Nucleic acids
c. Carbohydrates
d. Terpenes
e. Nucleotides

25. What is the ionic strength of a 0.5 M solution of Na_3PO_4?
a. 2.0 M
b. 1.5 M
c. 1.0 M
d. 0.5 M
e. 3.5 M

26. The ground state electronic configuration of a copper atom is best described by which of the following?
a. $[Ar]\ 4s^2\ 3d^9$
b. $[Kr]\ 4s^1\ 3d^{10}$
c. $[Ar]\ 4s^2\ 4d^9$
d. $[Kr]4s^1\ 4d^{10}$
e. $[Ar]\ 4s^1\ 3d^{10}$

27. Which of the following compounds would be most likely to react with NaI by way of the SN1 reaction mechanism?
a. Methyl bromide
b. Ethyl bromide
c. 2-bromo propane
d. 2-bromo-2-methyl propane
e. 2-bromo-2-phenyl propane

28. C^{14} has a half life of about 6000 years. Approximately how much of a 1 g sample of pure C^{14} would be left after 30,000 years?
    a. 0.5 g
    b. 0.19 g
    c. 0.03 g
    d. 0.015 g
    e. < 0.01 g

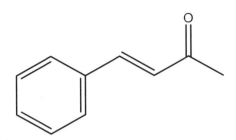

29. How many sp^2 hybridized atoms are in the molecule shown above?
    a. 5
    b. 10
    c. 6
    d. 8
    e. 4

30. A chemical reaction has the overall rate law of Rate = k[B][C]. If the initial concentration of both B and C is halved, what effect would this have on the reaction rate?
    a. The rate would remain unchanged
    b. The rate would be one half
    c. The rate would double
    d. The rate would be one fourth
    e. The rate would be on eighth

31. Which of the following is a strong Lewis acid?
    a. H_2SO_4
    b. Ph_3P
    c. $AlCl_3$
    d. HF
    e. AgCl

32. A chemical reaction has a ΔH° = 150 kJ/mol. Which of the following is true about this reaction?
   a. The reaction is endothermic
   b. The reaction is reversible
   c. The reaction is spontaneous
   d. The reaction is exothermic
   e. ΔS > 0

33. A compound has 5 chiral centers. What is the maximum number of stereoisomers possible for this compound?
   a. 10
   b. 5
   c. 25
   d. 32
   e. 16

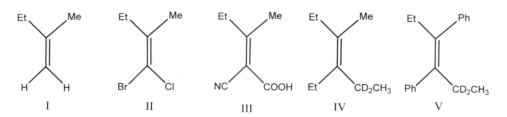

I   II   III   IV   V

34. Which of the above compounds is a Z alkene?
   a. I, II, III
   b. IV, V
   c. II, III
   d. II, IV
   e. II, V

35. The Bayer-Villager reaction converts
   a. Amides to esters
   b. Ketones to esters
   c. Ketones to acids
   d. Esters to aldehydes
   e. Acids to esters

36. If ^{238}Pu decays by α particle emission, what will the daughter product be?
   a. ^{237}Np
   b. ^{234}Pa
   c. ^{234}U
   d. ^{238}U
   e. ^{237}U

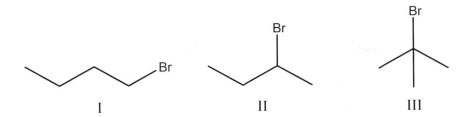

I   II   III

37. Place the compounds shown above in order of decreasing reactivity by way of the E2 mechanism:

- a. I>II>III
- b. III>II>I
- c. I>III>II
- d. II>I>III
- e. III>I>II

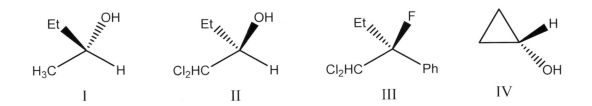

I   II   III   IV

38. Which of the molecules shown above is the R enantiomer of the compound?

- a. I, III, IV
- b. II, III
- c. I, II
- d. I, IV
- e. II,III

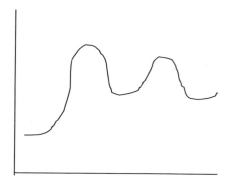

39. For the reaction above, place the products in order of increasing likelihood of formation.
    a. I>II>III
    b. III>II>I
    c. I>III>II
    d. II>I>III
    e. II>III>I

40. For the reaction energy diagram above, which of the following is true?
    a. Two intermediates, one transition state, ΔH is positive
    b. One intermediate, two transition states, ΔH is positive
    c. One intermediate, two transitions states, ΔH is negative
    d. Two intermediates, one transition state, ΔH is negative
    e. Two intermediates, two transition states, ΔH is positive

41. Which of the following elements are not known to have a stable isotope?
    a. Xe
    b. Os
    c. Sm
    d. Tc
    e. Cs

42. Place the bond types in order of increasing strength
    a. Ionic<dipole-dipole<London<hydrogen
    b. Covalent<London<dipole-dipole<hydrogen
    c. Hydrogen<London<ionic<dipole-dipole
    d. London<covalent<dipole-dipole<ionic
    e. London<dipole-dipole<hydrogen<covalent

- 134 -

43. Silicon doped with a trace of phosphorous is a material that is likely to be a
   a. Insulator
   b. Strong conductor
   c. N-type semiconductor
   d. P-type semiconductor
   e. I-type semiconductor

44. Which of the following is the most reactive acylating species?
   a. Ester
   b. Amide
   c. Anhydride
   d. Carboxylic acid
   e. Acid chloride

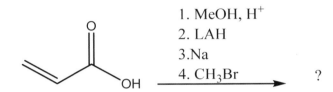

1. MeOH, H$^+$
2. LAH
3. Na
4. CH$_3$Br

?

45. What is the major organic product of the reaction sequence shown above?

   A.

   B.

   C.

   D.

   E.

$$CH_3Li \qquad CH_3SNa \qquad CH_3ONa \qquad CH_3COONa$$
$$\text{I} \qquad\qquad \text{II} \qquad\qquad\quad \text{III} \qquad\qquad\quad \text{IV}$$

46. Place the bases shown above in order of increasing basicity.
   a. I<II<III<IV
   b. IV<III<II<I
   c. II<III<I<IV
   d. II<I<III<IV
   e. IV<II<III<I

47. For an ideal gas held at constant pressure, which of the following statements must be true?
   a. A decrease in temperature must cause an increase in volume
   b. An increase in mass will lead to an increase in temperature
   c. An increase in volume will lead to a decrease in temperature
   d. A decrease in volume will lead to a decrease in temperature
   e. None of the above

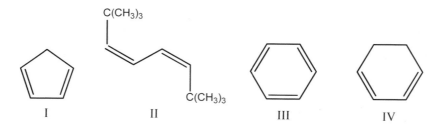

I   II   III   IV

48. Which of the compounds shown above would likely react very slowly *as dienes* in a Diels-Alder reaction?
   a. I and II
   b. II and III
   c. III and IV
   d. III
   e. II and IV

49. Brass is an alloy of which materials?
   a. Tin and copper
   b. Copper and iron
   c. Iron and tin
   d. Copper and zinc
   e. Zinc and tin

50. Two molecules might be diastereomers of each other if
   a. They are non-superimposable mirror images of each other
   b. They are constitutional isomers of each other
   c. They have a different formula
   d. They have the same formula and are not constitutional isomers
   e. Each has only one chiral center

Answers and Explanations

1. C. Electron affinity is the desire to obtain additional electrons. Na metal has no electron affinity and is eager to shed an electron and become Na^+. H^+ is quite stable, as is Cl^-. F has a strong electron affinity, but He^+ has the strongest, being a noble gas that has been ionized.

2. D. All of the mass measurements are off by nearly 10%, which can only be described as low accuracy. The measurements vary by only about a 0.1 g, which would be described as high precision.

3. E. All physical characteristics of enantiomers will be the same by definition.

4. A. The six fluorine atoms are arranged around the central sulfur atom at the points of a regular octahedron.

5. C. Strong electron donators tend to be ortho-para directors, while strong electron withdrawing groups tend to direct meta substitution.

6. C. An increase in pressure most certainly increases the boiling point and will also increase the melting temperature as well as the system tries to reestablish an equilibrium. Water is an exception as its melting temperature will decrease with increased pressure.

7. B. II is highly strained and will react quickly with electrophilic reagents to relieve that strain. III is highly hindered, greatly slowing reaction with electrophilic reagents.

8. B. Any process that increases the disorder or increases the number of particles will increase the entropy. Pure substances mixed together increases disorder, while separation of mixtures decreases disorder.

9. D. A and B are isomers of each other that differ in the connectivity of their atoms, therefore they cannot be stereoisomers of any kind. They are simply structural isomers, also known as constitutional isomers.

10. B. The Ksp is the solubility product, determined by the product of the concentrations of each ionic species. Since AgCl dissociates into Ag^+ and Cl^- equally, the square root of the Ksp must be the correct concentration, therefore B.

11. D. pH is equal to the −log of the $[H^+]$ concentration. Therefore, the $[H^+]$ concentration must be 10^{-4} M, or 0.0001 M.

12. A. According to Charles Law, the volume of an ideal gas will increase proportionately with an increase in temperature, or $V_1T_2 = V_2T_1$.

13. C. The reaction is an oxidation of an alcohol to an aldehyde. The best choice is C, chromium trioxide which will not over oxidize the alcohol when mixed with pyridine.

14. B. HF is the weakest, and acidity increases as you go down the column.

15. D. Proton signals are split into a number of peaks equal to the number of adjacent protons + 1. So "a" has no adjacent protons, and is therefore a singlet (0 + 1). "b" is adjacent to three protons (c), so the signal for "b" is a quartet. "c" is adjacent to two protons, and its signal will be split into a triplet.

16. B. All the others have $4n+2$ π electrons in an uninterrupted ring of sp^2 hybridized atoms.

17. B. Acetyl chloride will react quickly and violently with methanol to produce methyl acetate and HCl gas. Methanol will not react much at all with the other reagents.

18. A. The peak patterns of the two compounds would be very similar in proton NMR. All four other analytical tools would clearly distinguish the separate compounds.

19. C. Dividing the weight % by the atomic weights gives the correct ratio of atoms in the formula, which is 1:2 for C to H.

20. B. The Wittig reaction will produce a compound with a carbon-carbon double bond, but not a ring as in I.

21. C. Diamond and graphite are two different allotropes of carbon. They differ only in physical solid phase.

22. B. Normality refers to the concentration of acid equivalents. In this case, there are two per mol of sulfuric acid. Thus 2 x 0.25, or 0.5 N.

23. D. The ester portion is named first (methyl) followed by the description of the carboxylic acid portion, with the Cl on the -4- carbon of the chain.

24. E. DNA is composed of a double strand of nucleotide monomers. DNA itself is a nucleic acid.

25. A. The ionic strength is determined by adding the concentration of all the ionic components. In this case, 3 x 0.5 M for Na, and 1 x 0.5 M for PO_4, so 4 x 0.5 M = 2.0 M.

26. E. Copper has the inner configuration of argon, and the valence shell configuration of $4s^1 3d^{10}$. The second 4s electron occupies the 10th 3d position, giving a full d orbital and a half filled s orbital, which is more stable.

27. E. The SN1 reaction mechanism (substitution-nucleophilic unimolecular) requires an intermediate carbocation, which is favored by more highly substituted compounds. An adjacent phenyl ring is highly stabilizing towards carbocations, making (E) by far the most reactive.

28. C. 30,000 years would be 5 half lives of C^{14}. Therefore, the amount of C^{14} would have been halved 5 times, leaving 0.031 g.

29. B. Each double bond has two sp^2 hybridized atoms, or 10 atoms total.

30. D. By halving each concentration, the rate would be one fourth the original. Since the original rate was Rate = k[A][B], the new rate would be Rate = k[A/2][B/2] = k[A][B]/4.

31. C. Lewis acids are strong electron pair acceptors, and must have an empty valence orbital available to accept a lone pair from another molecule.

32. A. A positive heat of reaction indicates the reaction absorbs energy from the environment and is endothermic.

33. D. The maximum number of stereoisomers is 2^x, where x is the number of chiral centers.

34. C. The highest ranking ligand on each end of the double bond must be on the same face of the double bond to be Z. Et outranks Me, and Br outranks Cl. CN outranks COOH, CD_2CH_3 outranks Et, and Ph outranks Et and CD_2CH_3.

35. B. The Bayer-Villager reaction oxidizes ketones to esters with a peroxide reagent.

36. C. An alpha particle is a helium nucleus, which is composed of two protons and two neutrons. Therefore, the daughter product must have a mass 4 units fewer, and have two fewer protons, so the product must be ^{234}U.

37. B. The E2 mechanism (elimination bimolecular) favors more substituted alkyl halides.

38. C. Both I and II are the R enantiomers of their respective compounds. III is S and IV is not even chiral.

39. A. Free radical bromination favors the more substituted products over the less substituted products.

40. B. The humps represent transition states, the valley in the middle represents an intermediate, and the end of the reaction is higher than the beginning, therefore ΔH is positive.

41. D. Technetium is the earliest element in the periodic table without a stable isotope.

42. E. Both covalent and ionic are tremendously stronger than the intermolecular bonds such as London, dipole-dipole and hydrogen. London is the weakest and hydrogen is the strongest of the intermolecular bonds.

43. C. Phosphorous has an extra electron in the crystalline lattice available for generating a current. This is called a "negative semiconductor, or an N-semiconductor.

44. E. The acid chloride is the most reactive, because it produces the greatest partial positive charge on the carbonyl carbon center.

45. A. Step 1 forms the methyl ester. Step 2 reduces the ester to an alcohol. Step three forms the sodium salt of the alcohol. Step 4 produces the methyl ether of the alcohol. The double bond never reacts during the sequence.

46. E. IV is the least basic because the charge on oxygen is resonance stabilized. I is the most basic, as carbon has no ability to stabilize a negative charge. II is less basic than III because the negative charge is dispersed over the large sulfur atom.

47. D. With pressure constant, temperature and volume increase or decrease together.

48. B. II would not be able to attain the required s-cis conformation, and III is aromatic, so it would be unlikely to want to break that stable electronic configuration.

49. D. Alloys are solid state solutions of one metal with another. Brass is a mixture of copper and zinc. The properties of the alloy depend on the proportions of the metals in the mixture.

50. D. All stereoisomers must have the same formula and the same constitution.

Secret Key #1 - Time is Your Greatest Enemy

Pace Yourself

Wear a watch. At the beginning of the test, check the time (or start a chronometer on your watch to count the minutes), and check the time after every few questions to make sure you are "on schedule."

If you are forced to speed up, do it efficiently. Usually one or more answer choices can be eliminated without too much difficulty. Above all, don't panic. Don't speed up and just begin guessing at random choices. By pacing yourself, and continually monitoring your progress against your watch, you will always know exactly how far ahead or behind you are with your available time. If you find that you are one minute behind on the test, don't skip one question without spending any time on it, just to catch back up. Take 15 fewer seconds on the next four questions, and after four questions you'll have caught back up. Once you catch back up, you can continue working each problem at your normal pace.

Furthermore, don't dwell on the problems that you were rushed on. If a problem was taking up too much time and you made a hurried guess, it must be difficult. The difficult questions are the ones you are most likely to miss anyway, so it isn't a big loss. It is better to end with more time than you need than to run out of time.

Lastly, sometimes it is beneficial to slow down if you are constantly getting ahead of time. You are always more likely to catch a careless mistake by working more slowly than quickly, and among very high-scoring test takers (those who are likely to have lots of time left over), careless errors affect the score more than mastery of material.

Secret Key #2 - Practice Smarter, Not Harder

Many test takers delay the test preparation process because they dread the awful amounts of practice time they think necessary to succeed on the test. We have refined an effective method that will take you only a fraction of the time.

There are a number of "obstacles" in your way to succeed. Among these are answering questions, finishing in time, and mastering test-taking strategies. All must be executed on the day of the test at peak performance, or your score will suffer. The test is a mental marathon that has a large impact on your future.

Just like a marathon runner, it is important to work your way up to the full challenge. So first you just worry about questions, and then time, and finally strategy:

Success Strategy

1. Find a good source for practice tests.
2. If you are willing to make a larger time investment, consider using more than one study guide- often the different approaches of multiple authors will help you "get" difficult concepts.
3. Take a practice test with no time constraints, with all study helps "open book." Take your time with questions and focus on applying strategies.
4. Take a practice test with time constraints, with all guides "open book."
5. Take a final practice test with no open material and time limits

If you have time to take more practice tests, just repeat step 5. By gradually exposing yourself to the full rigors of the test environment, you will condition your mind to the stress of test day and maximize your success.

Secret Key #3 - Prepare, Don't Procrastinate

Let me state an obvious fact: if you take the test three times, you will get three different scores. This is due to the way you feel on test day, the level of preparedness you have, and, despite the test writers' claims to the contrary, some tests WILL be easier for you than others.

Since your future depends so much on your score, you should maximize your chances of success. In order to maximize the likelihood of success, you've got to prepare in advance. This means taking practice tests and spending time learning the information and test taking strategies you will need to succeed.

Never take the test as a "practice" test, expecting that you can just take it again if you need to. Feel free to take sample tests on your own, but when you go to take the official test, be prepared, be focused, and do your best the first time!

Secret Key #4 - Test Yourself

Everyone knows that time is money. There is no need to spend too much of your time or too little of your time preparing for the test. You should only spend as much of your precious time preparing as is necessary for you to get the score you need.

Once you have taken a practice test under real conditions of time constraints, then you will know if you are ready for the test or not.

If you have scored extremely high the first time that you take the practice test, then there is not much point in spending countless hours studying. You are already there.

- 145 -

Benchmark your abilities by retaking practice tests and seeing how much you have improved. Once you score high enough to guarantee success, then you are ready.

If you have scored well below where you need, then knuckle down and begin studying in earnest. Check your improvement regularly through the use of practice tests under real conditions. Above all, don't worry, panic, or give up. The key is perseverance!

Then, when you go to take the test, remain confident and remember how well you did on the practice tests. If you can score high enough on a practice test, then you can do the same on the real thing.

General Strategies

The most important thing you can do is to ignore your fears and jump into the test immediately- do not be overwhelmed by any strange-sounding terms. You have to jump into the test like jumping into a pool- all at once is the easiest way.

Make Predictions

As you read and understand the question, try to guess what the answer will be. Remember that several of the answer choices are wrong, and once you begin reading them, your mind will immediately become cluttered with answer choices designed to throw you off. Your mind is typically the most focused immediately after you have read the question and digested its contents. If you can, try to predict what the correct answer will be.

You may be surprised at what you can predict.

Quickly scan the choices and see if your prediction is in the listed answer choices. If it is, then you can be quite confident that you have the right answer. It still won't hurt to check the other answer choices, but most of the time, you've got it!

Answer the Question

It may seem obvious to only pick answer choices that answer the question, but the test writers can create some excellent answer choices that are wrong. Don't pick an answer just because it sounds right, or you believe it to be true. It MUST answer the question. Once you've made your selection, always go back and check it against the question and make sure that you didn't misread the question, and the answer choice does answer the question posed.

Benchmark

After you read the first answer choice, decide if you think it sounds correct or not. If it doesn't, move on to the next answer choice. If it does, mentally mark that answer choice. This doesn't mean that you've definitely selected it as your answer choice, it just means that it's the best you've seen thus far. Go ahead and read the next choice. If the next choice is worse than the one you've already selected, keep going to the next answer choice. If the next choice is better than the choice you've already selected, mentally mark the new answer choice as your best guess.

The first answer choice that you select becomes your standard. Every other answer choice must be benchmarked against that standard. That choice is correct until proven otherwise by another answer choice beating it out. Once you've decided that no other answer choice seems as good, do one final check to ensure that your answer choice answers the question posed.

Valid Information

Don't discount any of the information provided in the question. Every piece of information may be necessary to determine the correct answer. None of the information in the question is there to throw you off (while the answer choices will certainly have information to throw you off). If two seemingly unrelated topics are discussed, don't ignore either. You can be confident there is a relationship, or it wouldn't be included in the question, and you are probably going to have to determine what is that relationship to find the answer.

Avoid "Fact Traps"

Don't get distracted by a choice that is factually true. Your search is for the answer that answers the question. Stay focused and don't fall for an answer that is true but incorrect. Always go back to the question and make sure you're choosing an answer that actually answers the question and is not just a true statement. An answer can be factually correct, but it MUST answer the question asked. Additionally, two answers can both be seemingly correct, so be sure to read all of the answer choices, and make

sure that you get the one that BEST answers the question.

Milk the Question

Some of the questions may throw you completely off. They might deal with a subject you have not been exposed to, or one that you haven't reviewed in years. While your lack of knowledge about the subject will be a hindrance, the question itself can give you many clues that will help you find the correct answer. Read the question carefully and look for clues. Watch particularly for adjectives and nouns describing difficult terms or words that you don't recognize. Regardless of if you completely understand a word or not, replacing it with a synonym either provided or one you more familiar with may help you to understand what the questions are asking. Rather than wracking your mind about specific detailed information concerning a difficult term or word, try to use mental substitutes that are easier to understand.

The Trap of Familiarity

Don't just choose a word because you recognize it. On difficult questions, you may not recognize a number of words in the answer choices. The test writers don't put "make-believe" words on the test; so don't think that just because you only recognize all the words in one answer choice means that answer choice must be correct. If you only recognize words in one answer choice, then focus on that one. Is it correct? Try your best to determine if it is correct. If it is, that is great, but if it doesn't, eliminate it. Each word and answer choice you eliminate increases your chances of getting the question correct, even if you then have to guess among the unfamiliar choices.

Eliminate Answers

Eliminate choices as soon as you realize they are wrong. But be careful! Make sure you consider all of the possible answer choices. Just because one appears right, doesn't mean that the next one won't be even better! The test writers will usually put more than one good answer choice for every question, so read all of them. Don't worry if you are stuck between two that seem right. By getting down to just two remaining possible choices, your odds are now 50/50. Rather than wasting too much time, play the odds. You are guessing, but guessing wisely, because you've been able to knock out some of the answer choices that you know are wrong. If you are eliminating choices and realize that the last answer choice you are left with is also obviously wrong, don't panic. Start over and consider each choice again. There may easily be something that you missed the first time and will realize on the second pass.

Tough Questions

If you are stumped on a problem or it appears too hard or too difficult, don't waste time. Move on! Remember though, if you can quickly check for obviously incorrect answer choices, your chances of guessing correctly are greatly improved. Before you completely give up, at least try to knock out a couple of possible answers. Eliminate what you can and then guess at the remaining answer choices before moving on.

Brainstorm

If you get stuck on a difficult question, spend a few seconds quickly brainstorming. Run through the complete list of possible answer choices. Look at each choice and ask yourself, "Could this answer the question satisfactorily?" Go through each answer choice and consider it independently of the other. By systematically going through all possibilities, you may find something that you would otherwise overlook. Remember that when you get stuck, it's important to try to keep moving.

Read Carefully

Understand the problem. Read the question and answer choices carefully. Don't miss the question because you misread the terms. You have plenty of time to read each question thoroughly and make sure you understand what is being asked. Yet a happy medium must be attained, so don't waste too much time. You must read carefully, but efficiently.

Face Value

When in doubt, use common sense. Always accept the situation in the problem at face value. Don't read too much into it. These problems will not require you to make huge leaps of logic. The test writers aren't trying to throw you off with a cheap trick. If you have to go beyond creativity and make a leap of logic in order to have an answer choice answer the question, then you should look at the other answer choices. Don't overcomplicate the problem by creating theoretical relationships or explanations that will warp time or space. These are normal problems rooted in reality. It's just that the applicable relationship or explanation may not be readily apparent and you have to figure things out. Use your common sense to interpret anything that isn't clear.

Prefixes

If you're having trouble with a word in the question or answer choices, try dissecting it. Take advantage of every clue that the word might include. Prefixes and suffixes can be a huge help. Usually they allow you to determine a basic meaning. Pre- means before, post- means after, pro - is positive, de- is negative. From these prefixes and suffixes, you can get an idea of the general meaning of the word and try to put it into context. Beware though of any traps. Just because con is the opposite of pro, doesn't necessarily mean congress is the opposite of progress!

Hedge Phrases

Watch out for critical "hedge" phrases, such as likely, may, can, will often, sometimes, often, almost, mostly, usually, generally, rarely, sometimes. Question writers insert these hedge phrases to cover every possibility. Often an answer choice will be wrong simply because it leaves no room for exception. Avoid answer choices that have definitive words like "exactly," and "always".

Switchback Words

Stay alert for "switchbacks". These are the words and phrases frequently used to alert you to shifts in thought. The most common switchback word is "but". Others include although, however, nevertheless, on the other hand, even though, while, in spite of, despite, regardless of.

New Information

Correct answer choices will rarely have completely new information included. Answer choices typically are straightforward reflections of the material asked about and will directly relate to the question. If a new piece of information is included in an answer choice that doesn't even seem to relate to the topic being asked about, then that answer choice is likely incorrect. All of the information needed to answer the question is usually provided for you, and so you should not have to make guesses that are unsupported or choose answer choices that require unknown information that cannot be reasoned on its own.

Time Management

On technical questions, don't get lost on the technical terms. Don't spend too much time on any one question. If you don't know what a term means, then since you don't have a dictionary, odds are you aren't going to get much further. You should immediately recognize terms as whether or not you know them. If you don't, work with the other clues that you have, the other answer choices and terms provided, but don't waste too much time trying to figure out a difficult term.

Contextual Clues

Look for contextual clues. An answer can

be right but not correct. The contextual clues will help you find the answer that is most right and is correct. Understand the context in which a phrase or statement is made. This will help you make important distinctions.

Don't Panic

Panicking will not answer any questions for you. Therefore, it isn't helpful. When you first see the question, if your mind goes blank, take a deep breath. Force yourself to mechanically go through the steps of solving the problem and using the strategies you've learned.

Pace Yourself

Don't get clock fever. It's easy to be overwhelmed when you're looking at a page full of questions, your mind is full of random thoughts and feeling confused, and the clock is ticking down faster than you would like. Calm down and maintain the pace that you have set for yourself. As long as you are on track by monitoring your pace, you are guaranteed to have enough time for yourself. When you get to the last few minutes of the test, it may seem like you won't have enough time left, but if you only have as many questions as you should have left at that point, then you're right on track!

Answer Selection

The best way to pick an answer choice is to eliminate all of those that are wrong, until only one is left and confirm that is the correct answer. Sometimes though, an answer choice may immediately look right. Be careful! Take a second to make sure that the other choices are not equally

obvious. Don't make a hasty mistake. There are only two times that you should stop before checking other answers. First is when you are positive that the answer choice you have selected is correct. Second is when time is almost out and you have to make a quick guess!

Check Your Work

Since you will probably not know every term listed and the answer to every question, it is important that you get credit for the ones that you do know. Don't miss any questions through careless mistakes. If at all possible, try to take a second to look back over your answer selection and make sure you've selected the correct answer choice and haven't made a costly careless mistake (such as marking an answer choice that you didn't mean to mark). This quick double check should more than pay for itself in caught mistakes for the time it costs.

Beware of Directly Quoted Answers

Sometimes an answer choice will repeat word for word a portion of the question or reference section. However, beware of such exact duplication – it may be a trap! More than likely, the correct choice will paraphrase or summarize a point, rather than being exactly the same wording.

Slang

Scientific sounding answers are better than slang ones. An answer choice that begins "To compare the outcomes…" is much more likely to be correct than one that begins "Because some people insisted…"

Extreme Statements

Avoid wild answers that throw out highly controversial ideas that are proclaimed as established fact. An answer choice that states the "process should be used in certain situations, if…" is much more likely to be correct than one that states the "process should be discontinued completely." The first is a calm rational statement and doesn't even make a definitive, uncompromising stance, using a hedge word "if" to provide wiggle room, whereas the second choice is a radical idea and far more extreme.

Answer Choice Families

When you have two or more answer choices that are direct opposites or parallels, one of them is usually the correct answer. For instance, if one answer choice states "x increases" and another answer choice states "x decreases" or "y increases," then those two or three answer choices are very similar in construction and fall into the same family of answer choices. A family of answer choices is when two or three answer choices are very similar in construction, and yet often have a directly opposite meaning. Usually the correct answer choice will be in that family of answer choices. The "odd man out" or answer choice that doesn't seem to fit the parallel

construction of the other answer choices is more likely to be incorrect.

Special Report: What Your Test Score Will Tell You About Your IQ

Did you know that most standardized tests correlate very strongly with IQ? In fact, your general intelligence is a better predictor of your success than any other factor, and most tests intentionally measure this trait to some degree to ensure that those selected by the test are truly qualified for the test's purposes.

Before we can delve into the relation between your test score and IQ, I will first have to explain what exactly is IQ. Here's the formula:

Your IQ = 100 + (Number of standard deviations below or above the average)*15

Now, let's define standard deviations by using an example. If we have 5 people with 5 different heights, then first we calculate the average. Let's say the average was 65 inches. The standard deviation is the "average distance" away from the average of each of the members. It is a direct measure of variability - if the 5 people included Jackie Chan and Shaquille O'Neal, obviously there's a lot more variability in that group than a group of 5 sisters who are all within 6 inches in height of each other. The standard deviation uses a number to characterize the average range of difference within a group.

A convenient feature of most groups is that they have a "normal" distribution- makes sense that most things would be normal, right? Without getting into a bunch of statistical mumbo-jumbo, you just need to know that if you know the average of the group and the standard deviation, you can successfully predict someone's percentile rank in the group.

Confused? Let me give you an example. If instead of 5 people's heights, we had 100 people, we could figure out their rank in height JUST by knowing the average, standard deviation, and their height. We wouldn't need to know each person's height and manually rank them, we could just predict their rank based on three numbers.

What this means is that you can take your PERCENTILE rank that is often given with your test and relate this to your RELATIVE IQ of people taking the test - that is, your IQ relative to the people taking the test. Obviously, there's no way to know your actual IQ because the people taking a standardized test are usually not very good samples of the general population- many of those with extremely low IQ's never achieve a level of success or competency necessary to complete a typical standardized test. In fact, professional psychologists who measure IQ actually have to use non-written tests that can fairly measure the IQ of those not able to complete a traditional test.

The bottom line is to not take your test score too seriously, but it is fun to compute your "relative IQ" among the people who took the test with you. I've done the calculations below. Just look up your percentile rank in the left and then you'll see your "relative IQ" for your test in the right hand column-

Percentile Rank	Your Relative IQ		Percentile Rank	Your Relative IQ
99	135		59	103
98	131		58	103
97	128		57	103
96	126		56	102
95	125		55	102
94	123		54	102
93	122		53	101
92	121		52	101
91	120		51	100
90	119		50	100
89	118		49	100
88	118		48	99
87	117		47	99
86	116		46	98
85	116		45	98
84	115		44	98
83	114		43	97
82	114		42	97
81	113		41	97
80	113		40	96
79	112		39	96
78	112		38	95
77	111		37	95
76	111		36	95
75	110		35	94
74	110		34	94
73	109		33	93
72	109		32	93
71	108		31	93
70	108		30	92
69	107		29	92
68	107		28	91
67	107		27	91
66	106		26	90
65	106		25	90
64	105		24	89
63	105		23	89
62	105		22	88
61	104		21	88
60	104		20	87

Special Report: What is Test Anxiety and How to Overcome It?

The very nature of tests caters to some level of anxiety, nervousness or tension, just as we feel for any important event that occurs in our lives. A little bit of anxiety or nervousness can be a good thing. It helps us with motivation, and makes achievement just that much sweeter. However, too much anxiety can be a problem; especially if it hinders our ability to function and perform.

"Test anxiety," is the term that refers to the emotional reactions that some test-takers experience when faced with a test or exam. Having a fear of testing and exams is based upon a rational fear, since the test-taker's performance can shape the course of an academic career. Nevertheless, experiencing excessive fear of examinations will only interfere with the test-takers ability to perform, and his/her chances to be successful.

There are a large variety of causes that can contribute to the development and sensation of test anxiety. These include, but are not limited to lack of performance and worrying about issues surrounding the test.

Lack of Preparation

Lack of preparation can be identified by the following behaviors or situations:

Not scheduling enough time to study, and therefore cramming the night before the test or exam
Managing time poorly, to create the sensation that there is not enough time to do everything
Failing to organize the text information in advance, so that the study material consists of the entire text and not simply the pertinent information
Poor overall studying habits

Worrying, on the other hand, can be related to both the test taker, or many other factors around him/her that will be affected by the results of the test. These include worrying about:

Previous performances on similar exams, or exams in general
How friends and other students are achieving
The negative consequences that will result from a poor grade or failure

There are three primary elements to test anxiety. Physical components, which involve the same typical bodily reactions as those to acute anxiety (to be discussed below). Emotional factors have to do with fear or panic. Mental or cognitive issues concerning attention spans and memory abilities.

Physical Signals

There are many different symptoms of test anxiety, and these are not limited to mental and emotional strain. Frequently there are a range of physical signals that will let a test taker know that he/she is suffering from test anxiety. These bodily changes can include the following:

Perspiring
Sweaty palms
Wet, trembling hands
Nausea
Dry mouth
A knot in the stomach
Headache
Faintness
Muscle tension
Aching shoulders, back and neck
Rapid heart beat
Feeling too hot/cold

To recognize the sensation of test anxiety, a test-taker should monitor him/herself for the following sensations:

The physical distress symptoms as listed above
Emotional sensitivity, expressing emotional feelings such as the need to cry or laugh too much, or a sensation of anger or helplessness
A decreased ability to think, causing the test-taker to blank out or have racing thoughts that are hard to organize or control.

Though most students will feel some level of anxiety when faced with a test or exam, the majority can cope with that anxiety and maintain it at a manageable level. However, those who cannot are faced with a very real and very serious condition, which can and should be controlled for the immeasurable benefit of this sufferer.

Naturally, these sensations lead to negative results for the testing experience. The most common effects of test anxiety have to do with nervousness and mental blocking.

Nervousness

Nervousness can appear in several different levels:

The test-taker's difficulty, or even inability to read and understand the questions on the test
The difficulty or inability to organize thoughts to a coherent form
The difficulty or inability to recall key words and concepts relating to the testing questions (especially essays)
The receipt of poor grades on a test, though the test material was well known by the test taker

Conversely, a person may also experience mental blocking, which involves:

Blanking out on test questions
Only remembering the correct answers to the questions when the test has already finished.

Fortunately for test anxiety sufferers, beating these feelings, to a large degree, has to do with proper preparation. When a test taker has a feeling of preparedness, then anxiety will be dramatically lessened.

The first step to resolving anxiety issues is to distinguish which of the two types of anxiety are being suffered. If the anxiety is a direct result of a lack of preparation, this should be considered a normal reaction, and the anxiety level (as opposed to the test results) shouldn't be anything to worry about. However, if, when adequately prepared, the test-taker still panics, blanks out, or seems to overreact, this is not a fully rational reaction. While this can be considered normal too, there are many ways to combat and overcome these effects.

Remember that anxiety cannot be entirely eliminated, however, there are ways to minimize it, to make the anxiety easier to manage. Preparation is one of the best ways to minimize test anxiety. Therefore the following techniques are wise in order to best fight off any anxiety that may want to build.

To begin with, try to avoid cramming before a test, whenever it is possible. By trying to memorize an entire term's worth of information in one day, you'll be shocking your system, and not giving yourself a very good chance to absorb the information. This is an easy path to anxiety, so for those who suffer from test anxiety, cramming should not even be considered an option.

Instead of cramming, work throughout the semester to combine all of the material which is presented throughout the semester, and work on it gradually as the course goes by, making sure to master the main concepts first, leaving minor details for a week or so before the test.

To study for the upcoming exam, be sure to pose questions that may be on the examination, to gauge the ability to answer them by integrating the ideas from your texts, notes and lectures, as well as any supplementary readings.

If it is truly impossible to cover all of the information that was covered in that particular term, concentrate on the most important portions, that can be covered very well. Learn these concepts as best as possible, so that when the test comes, a goal can be made to use these concepts as presentations of your knowledge.

In addition to study habits, changes in attitude are critical to beating a struggle with test anxiety. In fact, an improvement of the perspective over the entire test-taking experience can actually help a test taker to enjoy studying and therefore improve the overall experience. Be certain not to overemphasize the significance of the grade - know that the result of the test is neither a reflection of self worth, nor is it a measure of intelligence; one grade will not predict a person's future success.

To improve an overall testing outlook, the following steps should be tried:

Keeping in mind that the most reasonable expectation for taking a test is to expect to try to demonstrate as much of what you know as you possibly can.

Reminding ourselves that a test is only one test; this is not the only one, and there will be others.

The thought of thinking of oneself in an irrational, all-or-nothing term should be avoided at all costs.

A reward should be designated for after the test, so there's something to look forward to. Whether it be going to a movie, going out to eat, or simply visiting friends, schedule it in advance, and do it no matter what result is expected on the exam.

Test-takers should also keep in mind that the basics are some of the most important things, even beyond anti-anxiety techniques and studying. Never neglect the basic social, emotional and biological needs, in order to try to absorb information. In order to best achieve, these three factors must be held as just as important as the studying itself.

Study Steps

Remember the following important steps for studying:

Maintain healthy nutrition and exercise habits. Continue both your recreational activities and social pass times. These both contribute to your physical and emotional well being. Be certain to get a good amount of sleep, especially the night before the test, because when you're overtired you are not able to perform to the best of your best ability.

Keep the studying pace to a moderate level by taking breaks when they are needed, and varying the work whenever possible, to keep the mind fresh instead of getting bored. When enough studying has been done that all the material that can be learned has been learned, and the test taker is prepared for the test, stop studying and do something relaxing such as listening to music, watching a movie, or taking a warm bubble bath.

There are also many other techniques to minimize the uneasiness or apprehension that is experienced along with test anxiety before, during, or even after the examination. In fact, there are a great deal of things that can be done to stop anxiety from interfering with lifestyle and performance. Again, remember that anxiety will not be eliminated entirely, and it shouldn't be. Otherwise that "up" feeling for exams would not exist, and most of us depend on that sensation to perform better than usual. However, this anxiety has to be at a level that is manageable.

Of course, as we have just discussed, being prepared for the exam is half the battle right away. Attending all classes, finding out what knowledge will be expected on the exam, and knowing the exam schedules are easy steps to lowering anxiety. Keeping up with work will remove the need to cram, and efficient study habits will eliminate wasted time. Studying should be done in an ideal location for concentration, so that it is simple to become interested in the material and give it complete attention. A method such as SQ3R (Survey, Question, Read, Recite, Review) is a wonderful key to follow to make sure that the study habits are as effective as possible, especially in the case of learning from a textbook. Flashcards are great techniques for memorization. Learning to take good notes will mean that notes will be full of useful information, so that less sifting will need to be done to seek out what is pertinent for studying. Reviewing notes after class and then again on occasion will keep the information fresh in the mind. From notes that have been taken summary sheets and outlines can be made for simpler reviewing.

A study group can also be a very motivational and helpful place to study, as there will be a sharing of ideas, all of the minds can work together, to make sure that everyone understands, and the studying will be made more interesting because it will be a social occasion.

Basically, though, as long as the test-taker remains organized and self confident, with efficient study habits, less time will need to be spent studying, and higher grades will be achieved.

To become self confident, there are many useful steps. The first of these is "self talk." It has been shown through extensive research, that self-talk for students who suffer from test anxiety, should be well monitored, in order to make sure that it contributes to self confidence as opposed to sinking the student. Frequently the self talk of test-anxious students is negative or self-defeating, thinking that everyone else is smarter and faster, that they always mess up, and that if they don't do well, they'll fail the entire course. It is important to decreasing anxiety that awareness is made of self talk. Try writing any negative self thoughts and then disputing them with a positive statement instead. Begin self-encouragement as though it was a friend speaking. Repeat positive statements to help reprogram the mind to believing in successes instead of failures.

Helpful Techniques

Other extremely helpful techniques include:

Self-visualization of doing well and reaching goals
While aiming for an "A" level of understanding, don't try to "overprotect" by setting your expectations lower. This will only convince the mind to stop studying in order to meet the lower expectations.
Don't make comparisons with the results or habits of other students. These are individual factors, and different things work for different people, causing different results.
Strive to become an expert in learning what works well, and what can be done in order to improve. Consider collecting this data in a journal.
Create rewards for after studying instead of doing things before studying that will only turn into avoidance behaviors.
Make a practice of relaxing - by using methods such as progressive relaxation, self-hypnosis, guided imagery, etc - in order to make relaxation an automatic sensation.
Work on creating a state of relaxed concentration so that concentrating will take on the focus of the mind, so that none will be wasted on worrying.
Take good care of the physical self by eating well and getting enough sleep.
Plan in time for exercise and stick to this plan.

Beyond these techniques, there are other methods to be used before, during and after the test that will help the test-taker perform well in addition to overcoming anxiety.

Before the exam comes the academic preparation. This involves establishing a study schedule and beginning at least one week before the actual date of the test. By doing this, the anxiety of not having enough time to study for the test will be automatically eliminated. Moreover, this will make the studying a much more effective experience, ensuring that the learning will be an easier process. This relieves much undue pressure on the test-taker.

Summary sheets, note cards, and flash cards with the main concepts and examples of these main concepts should be prepared in advance of the actual studying time. A topic should never be eliminated from this process. By omitting a topic because it isn't expected to be on the test is only setting up the test-taker for anxiety should it actually appear on the exam. Utilize the course syllabus for laying out the topics that should be studied. Carefully go over the notes that were made in class, paying special attention to any of the issues that the professor took special care to emphasize while lecturing in class. In the textbooks, use the chapter review, or if possible, the chapter tests, to begin your review.

It may even be possible to ask the instructor what information will be covered on the exam, or what the format of the exam will be (for example, multiple choice, essay, free form, true-false). Additionally, see if it is possible to find out how many questions will be on the test. If a review sheet or sample test has been offered by the professor, make good use of it, above anything else, for the preparation for the test. Another great resource for getting to know the examination is reviewing tests from previous semesters. Use these tests to review, and aim to achieve a 100% score on each of the possible topics. With a few exceptions, the goal that you set for yourself is the highest one that you will reach.

Take all of the questions that were assigned as homework, and rework them to any other possible course material. The more problems reworked, the more skill and confidence will form as a result. When forming the solution to a problem, write out each of the steps. Don't simply do head work. By doing as many steps on paper as possible, much clarification and therefore confidence will be formed. Do this with as many homework problems as possible, before checking the answers. By checking the answer after each problem, a reinforcement will exist, that will not be on the exam. Study situations should be as exam-like as possible, to prime the test-taker's system for the experience. By waiting to check the answers at the end, a psychological advantage will be formed, to decrease the stress factor.

Another fantastic reason for not cramming is the avoidance of confusion in concepts, especially when it comes to mathematics. 8-10 hours of study will become one hundred percent more effective if it is spread out over a week or at least several days, instead of doing it all in one sitting. Recognize that the human brain requires time in order to assimilate new material, so frequent breaks and a span of study time over several days will be much more beneficial.

Additionally, don't study right up until the point of the exam. Studying should stop a minimum of one hour before the exam begins. This allows the brain to rest and put things in their proper order. This will also provide the time to become as relaxed as possible when going into the examination room. The test-taker will also have time to eat well and eat sensibly. Know that the brain needs food as much as the rest of the body. With enough food and enough sleep, as well as a relaxed attitude, the body and the mind are primed for success.

Avoid any anxious classmates who are talking about the exam. These students only spread anxiety, and are not worth sharing the anxious sentimentalities.

Before the test also involves creating a positive attitude, so mental preparation should also be a point of concentration. There are many keys to creating a positive attitude. Should fears become rushing in, make a visualization of taking the exam, doing well, and seeing an A written on the paper. Write out a list of affirmations that will bring a feeling of confidence, such as "I am doing well in my English class," "I studied well and know my material," "I enjoy this class." Even if the affirmations aren't believed at first, it sends a positive message to the subconscious which will result in an alteration of the overall belief system, which is the system that creates reality.

If a sensation of panic begins, work with the fear and imagine the very worst! Work through the entire scenario of not passing the test, failing the entire course, and dropping out of school, followed by not getting a job, and pushing a shopping cart through the dark alley where you'll live. This will place things into perspective! Then, practice deep breathing and create a visualization of the opposite situation - achieving an "A" on the exam, passing the entire course, receiving the degree at a graduation ceremony.

On the day of the test, there are many things to be done to ensure the best results, as well as the most calm outlook. The following stages are suggested in order to maximize test-taking potential:

Begin the examination day with a moderate breakfast, and avoid any coffee or beverages with caffeine if the test taker is prone to jitters. Even people who are used to managing caffeine can feel jittery or light-headed when it is taken on a test day.
Attempt to do something that is relaxing before the examination begins. As last minute cramming clouds the mastering of overall concepts, it is better to use this time to create a calming outlook.
Be certain to arrive at the test location well in advance, in order to provide time to select a location that is away from doors, windows and other distractions, as well as giving enough time to relax before the test begins.
Keep away from anxiety generating classmates who will upset the sensation of stability and relaxation that is being attempted before the exam.
Should the waiting period before the exam begins cause anxiety, create a self-distraction by reading a light magazine or something else that is relaxing and simple.

During the exam itself, read the entire exam from beginning to end, and find out how much time should be allotted to each individual problem. Once writing the exam, should more time be taken for a problem, it should be abandoned, in order to begin another problem. If there is time at the end, the unfinished problem can always be returned to and completed.

Read the instructions very carefully - twice - so that unpleasant surprises won't follow during or after the exam has ended.

When writing the exam, pretend that the situation is actually simply the completion of homework within a library, or at home. This will assist in forming a relaxed atmosphere, and will allow the brain extra focus for the complex thinking function.

Begin the exam with all of the questions with which the most confidence is felt. This will build the confidence level regarding the entire exam and will begin a quality momentum. This will also create encouragement for trying the problems where uncertainty resides.

Going with the "gut instinct" is always the way to go when solving a problem. Second guessing should be avoided at all costs. Have confidence in the ability to do well.

For essay questions, create an outline in advance that will keep the mind organized and make certain that all of the points are remembered. For multiple choice, read every answer, even if the correct one has been spotted - a better one may exist.

Continue at a pace that is reasonable and not rushed, in order to be able to work carefully. Provide enough time to go over the answers at the end, to check for small errors that can be corrected.

Should a feeling of panic begin, breathe deeply, and think of the feeling of the body releasing sand through its pores. Visualize a calm, peaceful place, and include all of the sights, sounds and sensations of this image. Continue the deep breathing, and take a few minutes to continue this with closed eyes. When all is well again, return to the test.

If a "blanking" occurs for a certain question, skip it and move on to the next question. There will be time to return to the other question later. Get everything done that can be done, first, to guarantee all the grades that can be compiled, and to build all of the confidence possible. Then return to the weaker questions to build the marks from there.

Remember, one's own reality can be created, so as long as the belief is there, success will follow. And remember: anxiety can happen later, right now, there's an exam to be written!

After the examination is complete, whether there is a feeling for a good grade or a bad grade, don't dwell on the exam, and be certain to follow through on the reward that was promised...and enjoy it! Don't dwell on any mistakes that have been made, as there is nothing that can be done at this point anyway.

Additionally, don't begin to study for the next test right away. Do something relaxing for a while, and let the mind relax and prepare itself to begin absorbing information again.

From the results of the exam - both the grade and the entire experience, be certain to learn from what has gone on. Perfect studying habits and work some more on confidence in order to make the next examination experience even better than the last one.

Learn to avoid places where openings occurred for laziness, procrastination and day dreaming.

Use the time between this exam and the next one to better learn to relax, even learning to relax on cue, so that any anxiety can be controlled during the next exam. Learn how to relax the body. Slouch in your chair if that helps. Tighten and then relax all of the different muscle groups, one group at a time, beginning with the feet and then working all the way up to the neck and face. This will ultimately relax the muscles more than they were to begin with. Learn how to breathe deeply and comfortably, and focus on this breathing going in and out as a relaxing thought. With every exhale, repeat the word "relax."

As common as test anxiety is, it is very possible to overcome it. Make yourself one of the test-takers who overcome this frustrating hindrance.

Special Report: Retaking the Test: What Are Your Chances at Improving Your Score?

After going through the experience of taking a major test, many test takers feel that once is enough. The test usually comes during a period of transition in the test taker's life, and taking the test is only one of a series of important events. With so many distractions and conflicting recommendations, it may be difficult for a test taker to rationally determine whether or not he should retake the test after viewing his scores.

The importance of the test usually only adds to the burden of the retake decision. However, don't be swayed by emotion. There a few simple questions that you can ask yourself to guide you as you try to determine whether a retake would improve your score:

1. What went wrong? Why wasn't your score what you expected?

Can you point to a single factor or problem that you feel caused the low score? Were you sick on test day? Was there an emotional upheaval in your life that caused a distraction? Were you late for the test or not able to use the full time allotment? If you can point to any of these specific, individual problems, then a retake should definitely be considered.

2. Is there enough time to improve?

Many problems that may show up in your score report may take a lot of time for improvement. A deficiency in a particular math skill may require weeks or months of tutoring and studying to improve. If you have enough time to improve an identified weakness, then a retake should definitely be considered.

3. How will additional scores be used? Will a score average, highest score, or most recent score be used?

Different test scores may be handled completely differently. If you've taken the test multiple times, sometimes your highest score is used, sometimes your average score is computed and used, and sometimes your most recent score is used. Make sure you understand what method will be used to evaluate your scores, and use that to help you determine whether a retake should be considered.

4. Are my practice test scores significantly higher than my actual test score?

If you have taken a lot of practice tests and are consistently scoring at a much higher level than your actual test score, then you should consider a retake. However, if you've taken five practice tests and only one of your scores was higher than your actual test score, or if your practice test scores were only slightly higher than your actual test score, then it is unlikely that you will significantly increase your score.

5. Do I need perfect scores or will I be able to live with this score? Will this score still allow me to follow my dreams?

What kind of score is acceptable to you? Is your current score "good enough?" Do you have to have a certain score in order to pursue the future of your dreams? If you won't be happy with your current score, and there's no way that you could live with it, then you should consider a retake. However, don't get your hopes up. If you are looking for significant improvement, that may or may not be possible. But if you won't be happy otherwise, it is at least worth the effort.

Remember that there are other considerations. To achieve your dream, it is likely that your grades may also be taken into account. A great test score is usually not the only thing necessary to succeed. Make sure that you aren't overemphasizing the importance of a high test score.

Furthermore, a retake does not always result in a higher score. Some test takers will score lower on a retake, rather than higher. One study shows that one-fourth of test takers will achieve a significant improvement in test score, while one-sixth of test takers will actually show a decrease. While this shows that most test takers will improve, the majority will only improve their scores a little and a retake may not be worth the test taker's effort.

Finally, if a test is taken only once and is considered in the added context of good grades on the part of a test taker, the person reviewing the grades and scores may be tempted to assume that the test taker just had a bad day while taking the test, and may discount the low test score in favor of the high grades. But if the test is retaken and the scores are approximately the same, then the validity of the low scores are only confirmed. Therefore, a retake could actually hurt a test taker by definitely bracketing a test taker's score ability to a limited range.

Special Report: Additional Bonus Material

Due to our efforts to try to keep this book to a manageable length, we've created a link that will give you access to all of your additional bonus material.

Please visit http://www.mometrix.com/bonus948/grechemistry to access the information.